● Personal performa

● Elbæk (p.60)

Cognitive dissonance (p.56)
● Hard choice (p.74)

● Cognitive bias (p.76)
● Unimaginable (p.58)

● Making-of (p.68)   ● Energy (p.62)

Flow (p.52)   ● Personal potential trap (p.72)

● Political compass (p.64)

● Johari window (p.54)

THINKING

● A.I.(p.102)   ● Sinus/Bourdieu (p.94)

● Double-loop (p.98)   ● Maslow pyramids (p.92)

● Rumsfeld matrix (p.84)

● Pareto principle (p.104)

● Black box (p.118)

Prisoner's dilemma (p.120)

● Long-tail (p.106)

● Swiss cheese (p.88)   ● Black swan (p.112)

● Conflict resolution (p.108)
● Chasm (p.114)

THE DECISION BOOK

FIFTY MODELS FOR STRATEGIC THINKING

Mikael Krogerus
Roman Tschäppeler

Translated by Jenny Piening

WITH ILLUSTRATIONS BY PHILIP EARNHART

NEW, FULLY REVISED EDITION

PROFILE BOOKS

CONTENTS

Instructions for use   5

HOW TO IMPROVE YOURSELF
The Eisenhower matrix: *How to work more efficiently*   10
The SWOT analysis: *How to find the right solution*   12
The BCG box: *How to evaluate costs and benefits*   14
The project portfolio matrix: *How to maintain an overview*   16
The feedback analysis: *How you can learn to evaluate your own work*   20
The John Whitmore model: *Am I pursuing the right goal?*   22
The rubber band model: *How to deal with a dilemma*   24
The feedback box: *Dealing with other people's compliments and criticisms*   26
The Yes/No rule: *How to make a decision quickly*   28
The choice overload: *Why you should limit your options*   30
The gap-in-the-market model: *How to recognise a bankable idea*   32
The morphological box and SCAMPER: *Why you have to be structured to be creative*   34
The gift model: *How much to spend on presents*   38
Thinking outside the box: *How to come up with brilliant ideas*   40
The consequences model: *Why it is important to make decisions promptly*   42
The theory of unconscious thinking: *How to make decisions intuitively*   44
The Stop Rule: *When you should rethink a decision*   46
The buyer's decision model: *How to buy a car*   48

HOW TO UNDERSTAND YOURSELF BETTER
The flow model: *What makes you happy?*   52

The Johari window: *What others know about you*   54
The cognitive dissonance model: *Why people smoke when they know it's unhealthy*   56
The unimaginable model: *What do you believe in that you cannot prove?*   58
The Uffe Elbæk model: *How to get to know yourself*   60
The energy model: *Are you living in the here and now?*   62
The political compass: *What political parties stand for*   64
The personal performance model: *How to recognise whether you should change your job*   66
The making-of model: *To determine your future, first understand your past*   68
The personal potential trap: *Why it is better not to expect anything*   72
The hard choice model: *The four approaches to decision-making*   74
Cognitive bias: *The four mistakes we make in our thinking*   76
The crossroads model: *So, what next?*   78

HOW TO UNDERSTAND OTHERS BETTER

The Rumsfeld matrix: *How to analyse risks more effectively*   84
The Swiss cheese model: *How mistakes happen*   88
The Maslow pyramids: *What you actually need, what you actually want*   92
The Sinus Milieu and Bourdieu models: *Where you belong*   94
The double-loop learning model: *How to learn from your mistakes*   98
The AI model: *What kind of discussion type are you?*   102
The Pareto principle: *Why 80 per cent of the output is achieved with 20 per cent of the input*   104
The long-tail model: *How the internet is transforming the economy*   106

The conflict resolution model: *How to resolve a conflict
    elegantly*   108
The black swan model: *Why your experiences don't make
    you any wiser*   112
The chasm – the diffusion model: *Why everybody had an iPod*   114
The black box model: *Why faith is replacing knowledge*   118
The prisoner's dilemma: *When is it worth trusting someone?*   120

HOW TO IMPROVE OTHERS

The team model: *Is your team up to the job?*   126
The Hersey–Blanchard model (situational leadership):
    How to successfully manage your employees   128
The role-playing model (Belbin & de Bono): *How to change
    your own point of view*   132
The result optimisation model: *Why the printer always
    breaks down just before a deadline*   136
The project management triangle: *Why perfection is impossible*   138
The Drexler/Sibbet team performance model®: *How to turn
    a group into a team*   140
The expectations model: *What to consider when choosing a
    partner*   144
How will we decide in the future?   146

NOW IT'S YOUR TURN

Drawing lesson   152
Model lesson   154
My models   158

Bibliography   169
Thanks   172
Final note   173
The authors   174

INSTRUCTIONS FOR USE

WHY WE WROTE THIS BOOK

Nine years ago we were struck by the sudden realisation that we found it hard to make decisions. Not only big, life-changing decisions, but everyday ones, too: what to buy, what to wear, which music to download, what to order at the bar. So we went in search of models and methods that would help us to structure and classify, analyse and weigh up options – in other words, that would help us make decisions.

The result of our research is the book that you have in your hands. We wrote it primarily for ourselves. We thought that a print run of 500 would be more than enough. But then it sold a million copies in twenty languages. Obviously, other people were dealing with the same problem.

Over the years, we have received many useful suggestions of new models (and had mistakes in the book pointed out to us). So we decided to revise *The Decision Book* and to add some new decision-making theories.

WHY YOU SHOULD READ THIS BOOK

This book has been written for anyone who has to deal with people on a daily basis. Whether you are a teacher, a professor, a pilot or a top manager, you will be confronted by the same questions time and again: How do I make the right decision? How can I motivate myself or my team? How can I change things? How can I work more efficiently?

WHAT YOU WILL FIND IN THIS BOOK

The fifty best decision-making models – well-known and not so well-known – that will help you tackle these questions are described in words and diagrams. Don't expect straight answers; be prepared to be tested. Expect food for thought.

HOW TO USE THIS BOOK

This is a workbook. You can copy out the models, fill them in, cross them out, and develop and improve them. Whether you need to prepare for a presentation or carry out an annual performance review, whether a difficult decision lies ahead of you or a prolonged dispute is now behind you, whether you want to reassess your business idea or get to know yourself better – this book will guide you.

WHAT IS A DECISION-MAKING MODEL?

The models in this book fulfil the following criteria:

- They **simplify**: they do not embrace every aspect of reality, but only include those aspects that seem relevant.

- They **sum up**: they are executive summaries of complex interrelations.

- They are **visual**: using images, they convey concepts that are difficult to explain in words.

- They are **methods**: they do not provide answers, they ask questions; answers emerge once you have used the models, i.e. filled them out and worked with them.

WHY DO WE NEED DECISION-MAKING MODELS?

When we encounter chaos, we seek ways to structure it, to see through it, or at least to gain an overview of it. Models help us to reduce the complexity of a situation by enabling us to dismiss most of it and concentrate on what is important. Critics like to point out that models do not reflect reality. That is true, but it is wrong to claim that they compel us to think in a prescribed way. Models do not define what or how we should think; they are the result of an active thought process.

You can read this book in the American or the European way. Americans tend towards a trial-and-error approach: they do something, fail, learn from this, acquire theories and try again. If this approach suits you, start at the beginning with 'How to improve yourself'. Europeans tend to begin by acquiring theories, then doing something. If they then fail, they analyse, improve and repeat the attempt. If this approach is more your style, begin with 'How to understand yourself better' (p. 51).

Each model is only as good as the person who uses it.

HOW TO IMPROVE YOURSELF

THE EISENHOWER MATRIX

HOW TO WORK MORE EFFICIENTLY

The US president Dwight D. Eisenhower supposedly once said: 'The most urgent decisions are rarely the most important ones.' Eisenhower was considered a master of time management, i.e. he had the ability to do everything as and when it needed to be done. With the Eisenhower method, you will learn to distinguish between what is important and what is urgent.

Whatever the job that lands on your desk, begin by breaking it down according to the Eisenhower method and then decide how to proceed. We often focus too strongly on the 'urgent and important' field, on the things that have to be dealt with immediately. Ask yourself: When will I deal with the things that are important, but not urgent? When will I take the time to deal with important tasks before they become urgent? This is the field for strategic, long-term decisions.

Another method of organising your time better is attributed to the multimillionaire Warren Buffett. Make a list of everything you want to get done today. Begin with the task at the top of the list, and continue only when you have completed it. When a task has been completed, cross it off the list.

Better late than never. But never late is better.

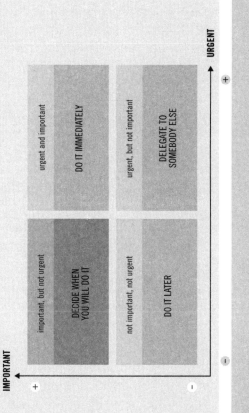

IMPORTANT

URGENT

important, but not urgent

DECIDE WHEN YOU WILL DO IT

urgent and important

DO IT IMMEDIATELY

not important, not urgent

DO IT LATER

urgent, but not important

DELEGATE TO SOMEBODY ELSE

Fill in the tasks you currently have to deal with.

THE SWOT ANALYSIS

HOW TO FIND THE RIGHT SOLUTION

With SWOT analysis, you evaluate the Strengths, Weaknesses, Opportunities and Threats identified in a project. The technique is based on a Stanford University study from the 1960s which analysed data from Fortune 500 companies. The study found a 35 per cent discrepancy between the companies' objectives and what was actually implemented. The problem was not that the employees were incompetent but that the objectives were too ambiguous. Many employees didn't even know why they were doing what they were doing. SWOT was developed from the results of the study to help those involved in a project to gain a clearer understanding of it.

It is worth taking the time to think about each step of the SWOT analysis rather than just hastily fill it out. How can we emphasise our strengths and compensate for (or cover up) our weaknesses? How can we maximise opportunities? How can we protect ourselves against threats?

What is interesting about SWOT analysis is its versatility: it can be applied to business and personal decisions with equal success.

If you're not failing, you're not trying hard enough. *Gretchen Rubin*

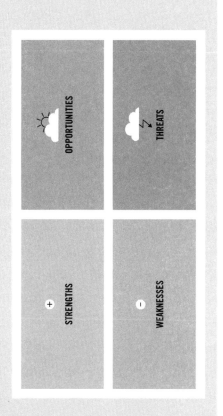

Think back to a big project in your life and about how you would have filled in a SWOT diagram at the time. Compare that with how you would fill it in today.

THE BCG BOX

HOW TO EVALUATE COSTS AND BENEFITS

In the 1970s, the Boston Consulting Group developed a method for assessing the value of the investments in a company's portfolio. The four-field matrix distinguishes between four different types of investment:

- **Cash cows** have a high market share but a low growth rate. This means they don't cost much but promise high returns. Consultants' verdict: milk them.

- **Stars** have a high market share and a high growth rate. But growth devours money. The hope is that the stars will turn into cash cows. Consultants' verdict: invest.

- **Question marks**, or 'problem children', have high growth potential but a low share of the market. With a lot of (financial) support and cajolement, they can be turned into stars. Consultants' verdict: a tough decision.

- **Dogs** are business units with a low share in a saturated market. Dogs should be held on to only if they have a value other than a financial one (e.g. a vanity project or favour for a friend). Consultants' verdict: liquidate.

The most dangerous words in investing are 'this time it's different.'
Sir John Templeton

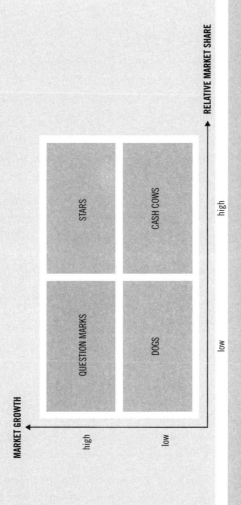

Arrange your financial products, investments or projects in the matrix. The axes indicate growth potential and market share.

THE PROJECT PORTFOLIO MATRIX

HOW TO MAINTAIN AN OVERVIEW

Are you juggling several projects simultaneously? Then you are a 'slasher' (/). The term was coined by the New York author Marci Alboher and describes people who cannot give a single answer to the question 'And what do you do for a living?'

Suppose you are a teacher/musician/web designer. The variety may be appealing, but how can you balance all these projects? And how do you ensure a regular income?

To get an overview, you can classify your current projects, both work-related and private, with the help of the project portfolio matrix according to cost and time (see model on pp. 18–19). Think of costs not only in terms of money but also in terms of resources such as friends involved, energy and psychological stress.

Cost and time are just two examples. You can use whatever parameters are relevant to your situation: for example, the x-axis could be 'How much my project is helping me achieve my overriding objective', and the y-axis 'How much I am learning from this project'. Now position your projects in the matrix in relation to the two axes 'objectives achieved' and 'amount learned'.

HOW TO INTERPRET THE RESULTS

- Reject projects if there is nothing you can learn from them and if they do not correspond to your overriding vision.

- Projects that you can learn from but do not correspond to your vision are interesting but will not help you achieve your objective. Try to change the project so that it serves your vision.

- If a project corresponds to your vision, but you are learning nothing new, look for somebody else to do it for you.

- If you are learning something and achieving your vision, you have hit the jackpot!

Make sure you complete your projects properly. Even those that aren't successful.

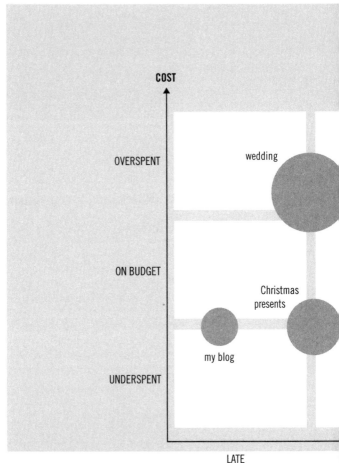

Arrange your current projects in the matrix: are you on budget and on time?

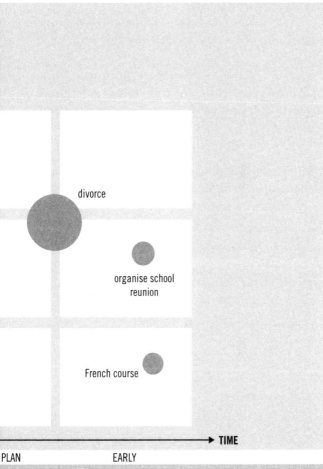

divorce

organise school
reunion

French course

→ **TIME**

PLAN   EARLY

THE FEEDBACK ANALYSIS

HOW YOU CAN LEARN TO EVALUATE YOUR OWN WORK

What is your greatest strength?

Most people think they know what they're good at, but they're usually wrong. So says Peter F. Drucker, one of the most important management thinkers of the last century. He came up with a simple yet clever technique for getting to know yourself better.

Whenever you have an important decision to make, write down what you expect to happen. After a year, compare your expectation with the actual outcome.

During his lifetime, Drucker continually compared his own expectations with the actual results. He learned to give himself feedback, and over time he began to recognise where and what kind of improvement was needed. Or to put it another way, he worked out where his strengths lay, and where they didn't.

Sounds easy? Calvinist ministers and Jesuit priests used this method as early as the mid-seventeenth century – and, according to some historians, the global impact of both religious orders is at least partially due to their use of feedback analysis, and using this technique to manage themselves.

Knowing what your strengths are is the most important thing an individual can know about himself or herself. *Peter F. Drucker*

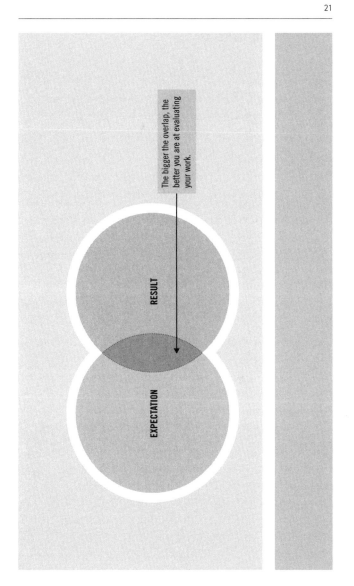

The bigger the overlap, the better you are at evaluating your work.

RESULT

EXPECTATION

THE JOHN WHITMORE MODEL

AM I PURSUING THE RIGHT GOAL?

If you set yourself goals, you should distinguish between final goals and performance goals. A final goal might be 'I want to run a marathon'; a performance goal helps you achieve this aim, for example 'I will go jogging for thirty minutes every morning'.

Write down your goal and check, step by step, whether it correlates with the fourteen requirements in the model.

A few things to note: if a goal is unattainable, there is no hope, and if it is not challenging it will not motivate you. If the fourteen steps are too complicated for you, keep in mind the following ground rule when establishing your goal:

KISS – Keep It Simple, Stupid!

The greatest danger for most of us is not that our aim is too high and we miss it, but that it is too low and we reach it. Michelangelo

➥ See also: Flow model (p. 52)

S	SPECIFIC		THE RIGHT GOAL	C	CHALLENGING
M	MEASURABLE	P	POSITIVELY STATED	L	LEGAL
A	ATTAINABLE	U	UNDERSTOOD	E	ENVIRONMENTALLY SOUND
R	REALISTIC	R	RELEVANT	A	AGREED
T	TIME-PHASED	E	ETHICAL	R	RECORDED

Once you have established a goal, check whether it correlates with these fourteen requirements.

THE RUBBER BAND MODEL

HOW TO DEAL WITH A DILEMMA

Is this a situation you are familiar with? A friend, colleague or client needs to make a decision that could irrevocably alter their future: for example to change career, move to another city or take early retirement. The arguments for and against are evenly balanced. How can you help them out of their dilemma?

Copy out the rubber band model, and ask the person to ask themselves: What is holding me? What is pulling me?

At first glance the method seems to be a simple variation of the conventional question 'What are the pros and cons?' The difference is that 'What is holding me?' and 'What is pulling me?' are positive questions and reflect a situation with two attractive alternatives.

A peacefulness follows any decision, even the wrong one.
Rita Mae Brown

➥ See also: SWOT analysis (p. 12)

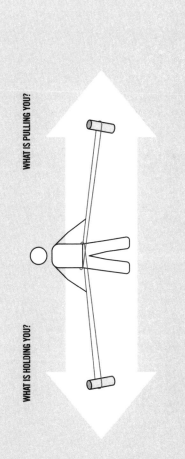

WHAT IS HOLDING YOU?

WHAT IS PULLING YOU?

If you have to decide between two good options, ask yourself what is holding you, and what is pulling you.

THE FEEDBACK BOX

DEALING WITH OTHER PEOPLE'S COMPLIMENTS AND CRITICISMS

Feedback is one of the most difficult and sensitive processes in groups. It is easy to hurt people with criticism, but false compliments are also unhelpful. Compliments often make us too complacent, while criticism damages our self-esteem and can lead us to make unwise choices.

The one-dimensional question 'What did you find good, what did you find bad?' is therefore not necessarily helpful. In terms of what can be learned from feedback, it is better to ask yourself 'What can I do with this criticism?' In other words, see what can stay as it is, and what needs to change (but may have been good up till now).

It is not only about working out what has not succeeded, it is also about deciding whether and how to react. The model will help you to categorise the feedback you receive in order to clearly establish a plan of action.

It is also important to ask yourself honestly: 'Which success or failure was in fact due to luck?' Were you the winner of a match because the ball found its way into the net purely by chance? Do you really deserve this compliment?

Pay attention to your thoughts, because they become words.
Pay attention to your words, because they become actions.
Pay attention to your actions, because they become habits.
Pay attention to your habits, because they become your character.
Pay attention to your character, because it is your fate.
From the Talmud

"I thought it was good, but it still needs to change!" **ADVICE**	"I thought it was good, and it can stay as it is in future!" **COMPLIMENT**
"I thought it was bad and it has to change!" **CRITICISM**	"I thought it was bad, but I can live with it!" **SUGGESTION**

Arrange the feedback you have received in the matrix. What advice do you want to follow? Which criticisms prompt you to take action? Which suggestions can you ignore?

THE YES/NO RULE

HOW TO MAKE A DECISION QUICKLY

A good way to quickly reach a decision is to use the Yes/No rule. It comes into its own when you have to weigh up risks, but have little time. Take the example of somebody who goes to the doctor feeling ill. The doctor makes a diagnosis based on a process of elimination (Does he have a fever? Is his blood pressure too low?).

The Yes/No rule is based on clear parameters, something that can be beneficial not only in medicine but also in management, private life or politics. In 2013, US president Barack Obama established three Yes/No rules to reach a decision about drone strikes: Does the targeted person pose a persistent and immediate threat to the American people? Is the USA the only country that can deal with this threat? Will civilians almost certainly not be harmed? Only if all three questions could be answered with a 'Yes' was a drone strike approved.

The oldest, shortest words – 'yes' and 'no' – are those that require the most thought.

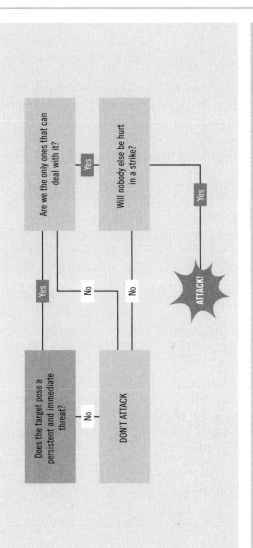

The former US president Barack Obama used this formula to decide for or against a drone strike.

THE CHOICE OVERLOAD

WHY YOU SHOULD LIMIT YOUR OPTIONS

Intuitively you might think that more means more. The more options we take into consideration, the better our final decision. The more choices we have, the happier we are. But sometimes the opposite is true: the greater the choice, the higher our expectations – and the more we worry that we will make the wrong decision. It is the so-called paradox of choice that the American business professor Sheena Iyengar demonstrated in a legendary experiment.

In a supermarket she offered a variety of jams for shoppers to try: six different varieties on one day, twenty-four varieties on another. With the smaller selection, 40 per cent tried the jams and 30 per cent bought a jar. The bigger selection attracted 60 per cent of the shoppers, but only 2 per cent bought a jar of jam. The conclusion: choice is alluring but confusing.

How do we solve this paradox of choice in our day-to-day lives? The psychology professor Barry Schwarz has a simple recommendation: reduce your choice. For example, in a restaurant, pick the first dish on the menu that you like the look of, and then immediately close the menu. Because the more options you juggle in your mind, the more dissatisfied you will be.

More is difficult.

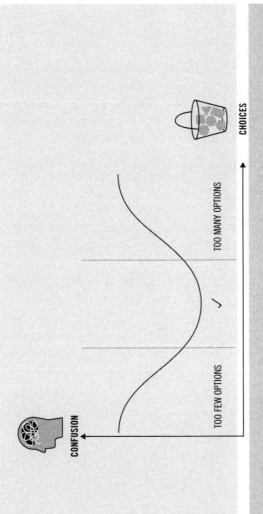

CHOICES

TOO MANY OPTIONS

TOO FEW OPTIONS

CONFUSION

Having no options makes us unhappy. So does having too many options.

THE GAP-IN-THE-MARKET MODEL

HOW TO RECOGNISE A BANKABLE IDEA

The goal of every new business is to discover and occupy a gap in the market. But what is the best way of proceeding? The gap-in-the-market model helps by depicting a market in a clear, three-dimensional way. Draw three axes that measure the development of your market, your customers and your future products.

Say that you want to open a new café. Position your competitors on the graph according to the following criteria:

- X-axis: Location (how much foot traffic does this street get?)

- Y-axis: Price (how expensive is the coffee?)

- Z-axis: Cool factor (how popular is the café?)

In areas that are dense with competitors, you should enter the market with your business model only if it has the potential to be a 'category killer'. (For example, by elevating coffee drinking from an ordinary, everyday habit to a premium experience, Starbucks became a category killer, and the benchmark for all other market players.) Look for a niche, an area that has been overlooked and that is not yet occupied.

Beware! If nobody else is in that area, you should check if there is any demand in the first place.

Positioning is like drilling for oil. Close is not good enough.

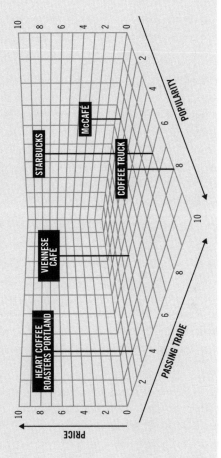

This model helps you to identify gaps in the market: position your competitors according to the three axes (e.g. pricing, potential for passing trade, popularity). Where is there a niche?

THE MORPHOLOGICAL BOX AND SCAMPER

WHY YOU HAVE TO BE STRUCTURED TO BE CREATIVE

Innovation can mean doing something completely new, but it can also mean making a new combination of things that already exist. But how is this achieved?

The concept of morphology stems from the study of biological structures and configurations. In the 1930s, the Swiss physicist Fritz Zwicky at the Institute of Technology in California developed a problem-solving method using what he called morphological boxes, in which a new entity is developed by combining the attributes of a variety of existing entities. This method, which was initially applied by Zwicky to jet engine technology, also began to be used in marketing strategies and the development of new ideas.

HOW IT WORKS

For the development of a new car, for example, all the relevant parameters (e.g. vehicle type, target group) are noted, and as many attributes as possible are ascribed to each parameter. This requires expertise as well as imagination, as the aim is to create something new out of something that already exists. The result of this method is a table (a morphological box can have up to four dimensions).

The next stage requires brainstorming: the car has to be an SUV, say, but it also needs to be energy-efficient and inexpensive to manufacture. Which attributes match these requirements? Connect your chosen attributes with a line. This gives you an overview of your priorities. Ask yourself: Could these attributes form the basis of a new car design? Or do you have to abandon some of them or add new ones?

Besides the morphological box, the SCAMPER checklist developed by Bob Eberle will also help you to reconfigure an existing idea or product. The following seven key questions are drawn from a questionnaire developed by Alex Osborn, founder of the advertising agency BBDO:

- **Substitute?** Substitute people, components, materials.

- **Combine?** Combine with other functions or things.

- **Adapt?** Adapt functions or visual appearance.

- **Modify?** Modify the size, shape, texture or acoustics.

- **Put to other use?** Other, new, combined uses.

- **Eliminate?** Reduce, simplify, eliminate anything superfluous.

- **Reverse?** Use conversely, invert, reverse.

The task is not so much to see what no one has yet seen, but to think what nobody yet has thought about that which everybody sees. Arthur Schopenhauer

➥ See also: Thinking outside the box (p. 40)

CONFIGURATION PARAMETERS	CONFIG. 1	CONFIG. 2
DESIGN (FRONT VIEW)	aggressive	angular (new edge)
PERFORMANCE, ENGINE	petrol 100–200 hp	petrol 200–300 hp
SEATS/ROOM	2	4
VEHICLE TYPE	saloon/sedan	mini-van
STYLE	confident	cool
FEATURES, MARKETING ASSETS	DVD player (cooperation with Netflix)	integrated music down from online stores
TARGET GROUP	HNWIs High Net Worth Individuals	DINKs Double Inco. No Kids

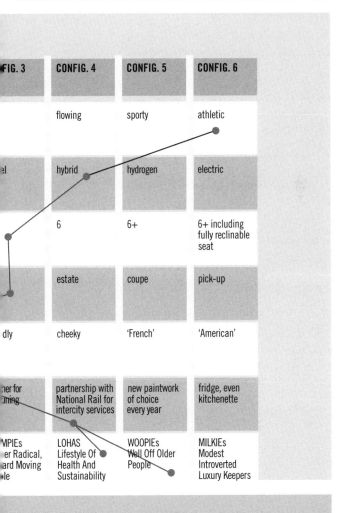

FIG. 3	CONFIG. 4	CONFIG. 5	CONFIG. 6
	flowing	sporty	athletic
el	hybrid	hydrogen	electric
	6	6+	6+ including fully reclinable seat
	estate	coupe	pick-up
dly	cheeky	'French'	'American'
ner for uning	partnership with National Rail for intercity services	new paintwork of choice every year	fridge, even kitchenette
MPIEs er Radical, ard Moving le	LOHAS Lifestyle Of Health And Sustainability	WOOPIEs Well Off Older People	MILKIEs Modest Introverted Luxury Keepers

THE GIFT MODEL

HOW MUCH TO SPEND ON PRESENTS

Gift-giving is something of a minefield. A cheap or impersonal gift can make the recipient feel undervalued, and create an awkward situation for both giver and receiver. Our highly unscientific little model has two axes:

- How expensive is the gift?
- How valued is it?

TWO RULES OF THUMB

Being generous beats being miserly (don't be misled by the sentence 'That really wasn't necessary').

The gift of an experience beats a material gift.

I have the simplest tastes. I am always satisfied with the best.
Oscar Wilde

EXPENSIVE

● LUXURY WATCH

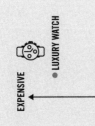

● GRANDFATHER'S
WATCH

● ATTENTION

→ VALUED

What is the most valued thing that you have ever received? And given as a gift?

THINKING OUTSIDE THE BOX

HOW TO COME UP WITH BRILLIANT IDEAS

A really innovative idea – rather than an old idea that has been applied to a new context, or a variation of an existing idea – is rare. Innovative ideas usually emerge when we leave our comfort zone, or when we break the rules. The example used here is the 'nine-point problem', which first appeared in puzzle magazines at the beginning of the twentieth century.

The task: Connect the nine points using a maximum of four straight lines without lifting your pen from the paper.

The solution: The trick is to extend the lines outside the box.

This puzzle is often used as an example of creative thinking. But don't jump to any rash conclusions – because Dr Peter Suedfeld, a professor of psychology at the University of British Columbia, made an interesting observation. He developed the Restricted Environmental Stimulation Technique (REST), which involves a person spending time in a darkened room with no visual or auditory stimulation. Suedfeld noticed that the subjects of the experiment didn't go mad. On the contrary: their blood pressure went down, their mood improved and they became more creative.

A person who wants to think outside the box is better off thinking inside a box.

➡ See also: Morphological box and SCAMPER (p. 34)

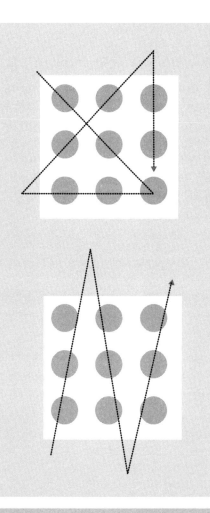

How to connect the nine points with a maximum of four lines.

THE CONSEQUENCES MODEL

WHY IT IS IMPORTANT TO MAKE DECISIONS PROMPTLY

We are often forced to make decisions based on limited or ambiguous information. At the beginning of a project, for example, when the finer details have yet to be clarified, we need to be bold in our decision-making – particularly because these early decisions have the most far-reaching consequences. Towards the end of a project we know more and have fewer doubts, but by then there is no longer anything fundamental to decide.

The most important question, then, is how we can bridge the chasm between doubt and decision.

Beware! We often defer decisions because we have doubts. But not making a decision is a decision in itself. If you delay a resolution it is often an unconscious decision, one that you do not communicate. This leads to uncertainty in a team. So if you want to make a decision later, be sure to communicate this clearly.

With this model, the Danish organisation theorists Kristian Kreiner and Søren Christensen encourage us to be courageous, and make decisions based on minimal information.

I'd rather regret the things I have done than the things that I haven't. *Lucille Ball*

➥ See also: Stop Rule (p. 46)

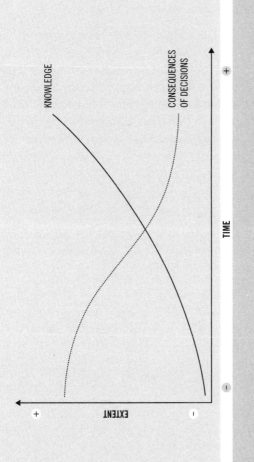

The model shows how the extent of the consequences of your decisions relates to the extent of your knowledge.

THE THEORY OF UNCONSCIOUS THINKING

HOW TO MAKE DECISIONS INTUITIVELY

It is tempting to believe that good decisions are the result of systematically thinking things through – and indeed, if the decision is a relatively straightforward one, impartially weighing up the pros and cons is likely to lead to the right outcome. However, if the decision is more complex and there doesn't seem to be an obvious answer, it is worth taking a break from thinking. Rather than trying to rationally weigh up all the arguments and information, trust your intuition. That may sound paradoxical, but the unconscious is better at sifting through large amounts of data.

But how do you turn off the rational side of your brain? The psychologist Gerd Gigerenzer suggests the following, intriguingly simple trick: if you can't decide between two options, toss a coin. While it is spinning in the air, you will probably sense which side you want to land face up. You then don't even need to look at the actual result.

The idea is to switch off the rational side of your brain and get in touch directly with your innermost desires and experiences. On the right you will find a second method.

Intuition is knowledge that we feel but cannot explain.

Method for making an intuitive decision
based on a method by Ap Dijksterhuis and Zeger van Olden

1. What is the decision you have to make?

   e.g. Shall I marry him?
   ....

   ....

2. Solve the following anagrams
   (anagram -> hint -> solution)

   TABLE → animal noise → BLEAT ....

   PLATE → flower part → ....

   SILENT → take notice → ....

   WARD → illustrate → ....

   SHORE → animal → ....

3. Now write down your decision.

   ....

   ....

This method is designed to stop the brain from thinking, so that the unconscious can be activated. Don't think about whether it's nonsense – just try it out!

THE STOP RULE

WHEN YOU SHOULD RETHINK A DECISION

In their excellent book *Simple Rules*, Kathleen Eisenhardt and Donald Sull argue that in certain situations, simple rules are more effective than complex ones because they shorten the amount of time needed to process information – one of the most time-consuming processes of all.

To give an example: How do I know when I should revise a decision? Give yourself a Stop Rule. The Stop Rule is a hard-and-fast, almost universally applicable alternative to the often tortuous process of weighing up a situation. In 1935, the legendary investor Gerald Loeb formulated a simple but powerful Stop Rule for the eternal question asked by all investors: When should I sell? Loeb's rule: if an investment loses 10 per cent of its value, sell it! No questions asked.

The beauty of Stop Rules like these is that they are unconditional. They prevent headaches – and can even save lives. Mountaineers use stop rules to ensure their safe return. For example: if we don't reach the summit by 2pm, we turn around. When such a Stop Rule was broken on Mount Everest in 1996, eight people died.

It is an art to recognise the boundaries between cowardice and madness. *Reinhold Messner*

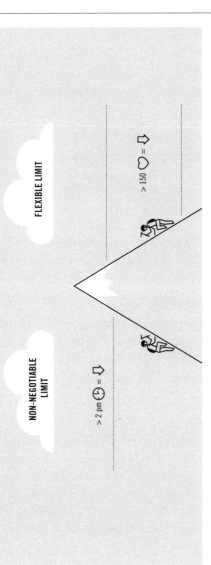

NON-NEGOTIABLE LIMIT

> 2 pm 🕐 = ⇨

FLEXIBLE LIMIT

> 150 ♡ = ⇨

Two variations of the Stop Rule: non-negotiable limit (if we don't reach the summit by 2pm, we turn around) and flexible limit (if my heart rate is still below 150 by 2pm, I will keep climbing until 3pm).

THE BUYER'S DECISION MODEL

HOW TO BUY A CAR

Let's say you want to buy a car, but can't make a decision. Four-and-half helpful hints:

1. Establish a research strategy.

The problem of research is that we never know enough but can quickly know too much. Nowadays, all it takes to acquire the same level of knowledge as a car dealer is a bit of internet research. And the more you know, the more secure you feel. But eventually you reach a tipping point; at some point you know too much. Theoretically you could spend the rest of your life reading car reviews. Here's what to do: set yourself your own limits, e.g. three hours on Google, ask three friends, visit two car dealers.

2. Lower your expectations.

Don't look for the perfect car: look for a car that fulfils your basic requirements. So says psychology professor Barry Schwarz. Even if it isn't the best choice, it can make you happier than no car at all or endlessly searching for one. Here's what to do: put your five most important criteria for the car in order of priority. Delete the last two.

3. Don't worry.

According to the psychologist Daniel Gilbert, most decisions are not as lasting as we might think in the moment of making them. Here's what to do: use the 10-10-10 technique of Suzy Welch, who graduated from Harvard in the top 5 per cent of her class. In relation to buying a car, ask yourself: What consequences will my decision have in 10 days? What consequences will it have in 10 months? And in 10 years?

4. Let somebody else decide.

Most people think it is better to make decisions themselves. However, Simona Botti from the London Business School, proved in an experiment that when making a decision ourselves we are often subject to nagging doubts that we didn't make the best possible choice. This doubt goes away if someone else decides for us. Here's what to do: if you're deciding between two relatively equal cars, let the seller make the decision for you.

Or you can follow the example of Ignatius of Loyola, co-founder of the Jesuit order: spend three days acting as if you had decided on option one, then spend three days acting as if you had decided on option two, and only then make a decision.

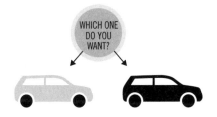

HOW TO UNDERSTAND
YOURSELF BETTER

THE FLOW MODEL

WHAT MAKES YOU HAPPY?

Over two thousand years ago, Aristotle came to the unsurprising conclusion that what a person wants above all is to be happy. In 1961, the American psychologist Mihály Csíkszentmihályi wrote: 'While happiness itself is sought for its own sake, every other goal – health, beauty, money or power – is valued only because we expect that it will make us happy'. Csíkszentmihályi looked for a term that described the state of feeling happy. He called it 'flow'. But when are we 'in the flow'?

After interviewing over a thousand people about what made them happy, he found that all the responses had five things in common. Happiness, or 'flow', occurs when we are:

- intensely focused on an activity
- of our own choosing, that is
- neither under-challenging (boreout) nor over-challenging (burnout), that has
- a clear objective, and that receives
- immediate feedback.

Csíkszentmihályi discovered that people who are 'in the flow' not only feel a profound sense of satisfaction, they also lose track of time and forget themselves completely because they are so immersed in what they are doing. Musicians, athletes, actors, doctors and artists describe how they are happiest when they are absorbed in an often exhausting activity – totally contradicting the commonly held view that happiness has to do with relaxation.

What is preventing you from being happy?

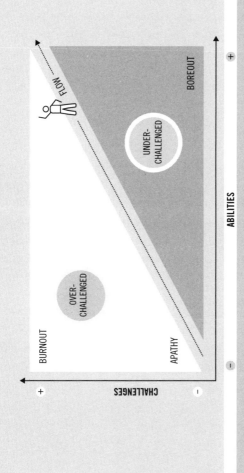

The model has two axes: the level of the challenge, and the level of your abilities. On the graph, write down the last three challenges you have faced, and how you felt about them.

THE JOHARI WINDOW

WHAT OTHERS KNOW ABOUT YOU

We cannot 'grasp' our own personality, but we can be aware of what part of our personality we reveal to the outside world. The Johari window ('Johari' is derived from the first syllables of the first names of its inventors, Joseph Luft and Harry Ingham) is one of the most interesting models for describing human interaction. A four-paned 'window' divides personal awareness into four different types:

A. This quadrant describes characteristics and experiences that we are aware of ourselves and that we like to tell others about.

B. This 'hidden' quadrant describes things that we know about ourselves but choose not reveal to others. It decreases in size the more we build up a trusting relationship with others.

C. There are things that we do not know about ourselves but that others can see clearly. And there are things that we think we are expressing clearly, but which others interpret completely differently. In this quadrant, feedback can be enlightening but also hurtful.

D. There are aspects of ourselves that are hidden from ourselves as well as others. We are more complex and multifaceted than we think. From time to time something unknown rises to the surface from our unconscious – for example in a dream.

Choose adjectives (fun, unreliable, etc.) that you think describe you well. Then let others (friends, colleagues) choose adjectives to describe you. The adjectives are then entered in the appropriate panes of the window.

Try this exercise with your partner. Are there things about your partner that you wished you had never discovered? And what do you wish you didn't know about yourself?

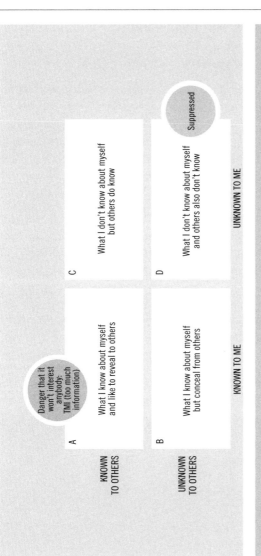

Danger that it won't interest anybody. TMI (too much information)

A
What I know about myself and like to reveal to others

C
What I don't know about myself but others do know

B
What I know about myself but conceal from others

D
What I don't know about myself and others also don't know

Suppressed

KNOWN
TO OTHERS

UNKNOWN
TO OTHERS

KNOWN TO ME

UNKNOWN TO ME

What do others know about you that you don't know yourself? The Johari window provides a model of personal awareness.

THE COGNITIVE DISSONANCE MODEL

WHY PEOPLE SMOKE WHEN THEY KNOW IT'S UNHEALTHY

There is often a big gap between what we think and what we do: when we do something despite knowing it to be immoral, wrong or stupid, we have a bad conscience. The psychologist Leon Festinger used the term 'cognitive dissonance' to describe our state of mind when our actions are not consistent with our beliefs – for example, when we make a decision that proves to be wrong, but we don't want to admit it.

But why do we find it so difficult to recognise our mistakes? Why do we even go as far as defending our actions when we are confronted with their shortcomings? Rather than asking for forgiveness, one of the more unlikeable human attributes kicks in: self-justification. This acts as a protective mechanism that enables us to sleep at night and frees us from self-doubt. We see only what we want to see, and ignore everything that contradicts our view. We look for arguments that reinforce our position.

But how can we overcome this dissonance? Either by changing our behaviour or our attitude.

A great nation is like a great man: when he makes a mistake, he realises it. Having realised it, he admits it. Having admitted it, he corrects it. He considers those who point out his faults as his most benevolent teachers. Lao Tzu

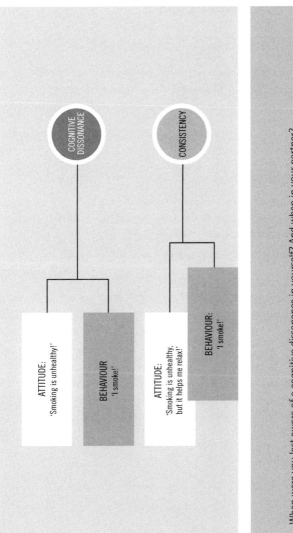

COGNITIVE DISSONANCE

ATTITUDE:
'Smoking is unhealthy!'

BEHAVIOUR
'I smoke!'

CONSISTENCY

ATTITUDE:
'Smoking is unhealthy,
but it helps me relax!'

BEHAVIOUR:
'I smoke!'

When were you last aware of a cognitive dissonance in yourself? And when in your partner?

THE UNIMAGINABLE MODEL

WHAT DO YOU BELIEVE IN THAT YOU CANNOT PROVE?

Models explain how everything is connected, how we should act and what we should and should not do. But do they prevent us from seeing things for what they really are?

As early as the eighteenth century, Adam Smith warned against being carried away by a love of abstract systems, and two centuries later Albert Einstein received a Nobel Prize for recognising that models and 'logical' systems are ultimately a matter of faith. The historian of science and philosopher Thomas Kuhn argued that science usually just works towards corroborating its models, and reacts with ignorance when – as is often the case – the models do not correspond to reality. This insight may not have earned him a Nobel Prize, but he did land himself a professorship at an elite university.

We often believe so strongly in models that they take on the status of reality. A good example of this is the ontological proof of the existence of God, which Kant explored in his philosophy. He maintained that if we are able to imagine a being as perfect as God, then he must exist. Ways in which we blindly accept models as 'reality' can also be found in our everyday lives: for example, if we are told that humankind is full of greed and egoism, this model of behaviour may be internalised and (unconsciously) imitated.

I hate reality but it's still the best place to get a good steak.
Woody Allen

➥ See also: Black box model (p. 118), How will we decide in the future? (p. 146)

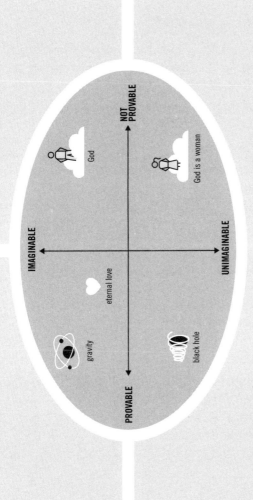

What do you believe in, despite not understanding the evidence? And what do you believe in despite having no evidence to support it?

THE UFFE ELBÆK MODEL

HOW TO GET TO KNOW YOURSELF

If you want to gain a general understanding of yourself and others, Uffe Elbæk's public opinion barometer is a good starting point. It reveals behavioural traits and tendencies.

You should bear in mind that you are always subject to four different perspectives:

- how you see yourself
- how you would like to see yourself
- how others see you
- how others would like to see you

PROCEED AS FOLLOWS

- Without taking time to think about it, decide the following on a scale of one to ten. How much of a team person are you, and how much of an individualist? Do you pay more attention to content or to form? What is more important to you: the body or the mind? Do you feel more global than local? Use a pen to connect the lines.
- Now take a different coloured pen to mark on the scale how you would like to see yourself.
- Define your own axes (rich–poor, happy–sad, extroverted–introverted).

Beware! You are only creating a snapshot. And note that the sum of an axis should always be ten (you cannot be ten points local and ten points global).

What is preventing you from being the way you would like to be?

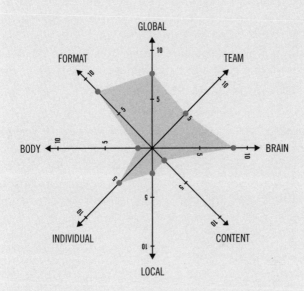

Fill in the model for yourself. Then ask your partner or a good friend to fill it in for you. Compare the results.

THE ENERGY MODEL

ARE YOU LIVING IN THE HERE AND NOW?

It is always said that we should live 'in the here and now'. But why? The Swiss author Pascal Mercier says this: 'It is an error, a nonsensical act of violence, to concentrate on the here and now with the conviction of thus grasping the essential. What matters is to move surely and calmly, with the appropriate humour and the appropriate melancholy in the temporally and spatially internal landscape that we are.'

Here is a non-judgemental question: How much of your time do you spend thinking about the past, how much about the here and now, and how much about the future? Or to put it another way, how often do you think, wistfully or thankfully, about what has been? How often do you have the feeling that you are really concentrating on what you are doing at a particular moment? How often do you imagine what the future may hold, and how often do you worry about what lies ahead of you?

The three examples shown in the model on the right can also represent cultural values: memory-driven, in nostalgic Europe; dream-driven, in the USA, the 'land of opportunity'; and reality-driven, in industrious Asia.

You can't change the past. But you can ruin the present by worrying about the future.

➥ See also: Crossroads model (p. 78)

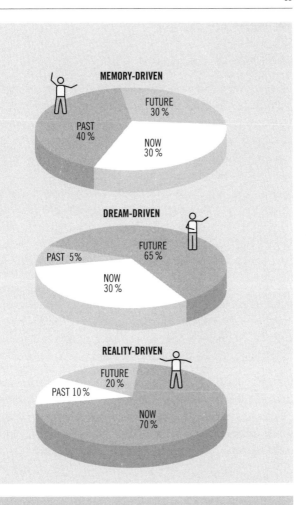

MEMORY-DRIVEN

FUTURE
30 %

PAST
40 %

NOW
30 %

DREAM-DRIVEN

FUTURE
65 %

PAST 5 %

NOW
30 %

REALITY-DRIVEN

FUTURE
20 %

PAST 10 %

NOW
70 %

Fill in how much time you spend in the past, present and future.

THE POLITICAL COMPASS

WHAT POLITICAL PARTIES STAND FOR

Although we still tend to think of politics in terms of 'left' and 'right', this polarisation is too simplistic to describe today's complex political landscape. In the UK, for example, despite being traditionally at opposite ends of the political spectrum, during the 2000s Labour and the Conservative party moved ever closer in terms of shared economic and social policies. Traditional definitions can also be misleading. UKIP is widely regarded as radically right-wing because of its position on nationalism, yet it is to the left of the Conservatives when it comes to some social issues. In the run-up to the 2017 General Election, Labour had leapt to the left of the Green Party, and the Liberal Democrats were on the side of authoritarianism.

The clear-cut political divisions of the past may have become blurred, but there are models for measuring the views and attitudes of voters. One of the most famous of these tools is called the political compass. You can plot your political position on this model, using its left–right and liberal–authoritarian axes.

Note that the left–right axis refers not to political orientation in the traditional sense, but to economic policy: left = nationalisation, right = privatisation. The liberal–authoritarian axis refers to individual rights: liberal = all rights lie with the individual, authoritarian = the state has a high degree of control over its citizens.

War does not determine who is right – only who is left.
Jessie Woodrow Wilson Sayre

AUTHORITARIAN

UKIP

DUP

Conservative

Scottish
Socialist Party

Liberal Democrat

Scottish National Party

LEFT

RIGHT

SDLP

Plaid Cymru

Labour

Green

LIBERTARIAN

Analysis of the UK political landscape at the time of the 2017
general election by politicalcompass.org. Ask yourself where you
stand. Where did you stand ten years ago?

THE PERSONAL PERFORMANCE MODEL

HOW TO RECOGNISE WHETHER YOU SHOULD CHANGE YOUR JOB

Many people are unhappy in their jobs. But how can job dissatisfaction be measured? This model will help you to evaluate your job situation.

Every evening for three weeks, ask yourself the following three questions, and insert your answers in the model on a scale of one ('doesn't apply at all') to ten ('totally applies'):

- **Have to.** To what extent are my current tasks being imposed on me or demanded of me?
- **Able to.** To what extent do my tasks match my abilities?
- **Want to.** To what extent does my current task correspond to what I really want?

After three weeks, analyse the shapes of the different 'sails'. If you are 'moving', then your job offers you variety. If the shape of the sail is always the same, then ask yourself the following:

- What do you want?
- Are you able to do what you want?
- What are you able to do?
- Do you want what you are able to do?

If you can't do something, you have to work at it.

➥ See also: Rubber band model (p. 24), Flow model (p. 52)

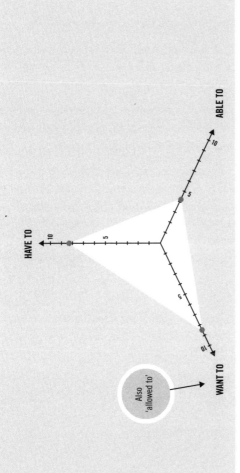

HAVE TO

ABLE TO

WANT TO

Also 'allowed to'

To what extent are your current tasks being imposed on you? To what extent do they match your abilities, and to what extent do they correspond to what you want?

THE MAKING-OF MODEL

TO DETERMINE YOUR FUTURE, FIRST UNDERSTAND YOUR PAST

When it comes to strategic decisions, we usually focus on the future. Our dreams are acted out in the future, and our hopes are pinned on fulfilling these dreams.

But why? Perhaps because we think we can determine our future. However, we tend to forget that every future has a past, and that our past is the foundation on which our future is built.

That's why the important question is not 'How do I imagine my future?' but 'How do I create a connection, a bridge, between the past (e.g. of a project) and the future?' This model, inspired by a visual planning system developed by The Grove consulting agency, helps you to work out what was relevant in your past and what you can forget, and what you should take with you from your past into the future.

This is how it works: you define a timeframe – e.g. the last year, your schooldays, your marriage, or from the founding of a company to today – and think back to the start of that period, either alone or in a group. Then add the following to the timeline:

- your goals (at the time)

- what you learned

- the obstacles you overcame

- the successes

- the people involved

The filled-in model reveals the importance you attach to your past.

Memory is the only paradise from which we cannot be driven.
Jean Paul

GOALS
(at the time)

 WHAT YOU LEARNED

 OBSTACLES
(that you overcame)

 SUCCESSES

 PEOPLE

Choose a timeframe and note the following:
What were your goals? What did you learn?
What obstacles did you overcome?

THE PERSONAL POTENTIAL TRAP

WHY IT IS BETTER NOT TO EXPECT ANYTHING

'Such a promising boy' – anybody who has heard this said about them can already guess what lies behind the personal potential trap: a lifetime of striving to fulfil this promise.

It is the curse of talented people. 'He just needs to find out what he really wants', people say. His shortcomings are overlooked and his successes admired for the ease with which they are achieved. To begin with, he profits from this attractive yet fatal combination of talent and charisma. That is, until the stupid ones become hard-working: then he has to watch from the sidelines as he is over-taken by precisely those people who had once enviously looked up to him.

The personal potential trap can be precisely traced. In the model are three curves:

- my expectations of myself

- other people's expectations of me

- my actual achievements

The trap opens as soon as others' expectations of you and your actual achievements diverge too much. Normally a talented person cruises along until a crisis point is reached. The way to go is to prom-ise 80 and deliver 120.

Are you prepared to expect less of yourself than you think others expect of you?

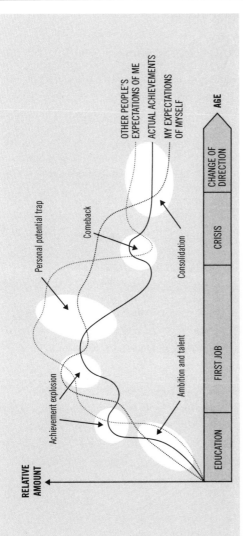

RELATIVE AMOUNT

OTHER PEOPLE'S EXPECTATIONS OF ME

ACTUAL ACHIEVEMENTS

MY EXPECTATIONS OF MYSELF

Personal potential trap

Comeback

Achievement explosion

Consolidation

Ambition and talent

EDUCATION | FIRST JOB | CRISIS | CHANGE OF DIRECTION

AGE

The model shows three curves: my own expectations, the expectations of others and my achievements. If the three diverge too much, you will fall into the personal potential trap.

THE HARD CHOICE MODEL

THE FOUR APPROACHES TO DECISION-MAKING

Technically speaking, every decision has two parameters: How comparable are the two options, and how great is the consequence of the decision? Arranged in a matrix, this results in four different outcomes:

1. Easy to compare, no consequence: One alternative is better than the other but it does not play a (big) role if we make the wrong decision.

2. Difficult to compare, slight consequence: Shall we go to the party or get an early night? The one option is better in one sense, the other in another, but they aren't really comparable. This makes the decision difficult, even if it isn't actually that important.

3. Easy to compare, big consequence: When we discover that there is only one operation that could save our life, we face a big decision – but it is easy to make, because there is no real alternative.

4. Difficult to compare, big consequence: Starting a family, changing job – with these hard choices there is no obviously right decision. According to the philosopher Ruth Chang, whatever decision you make in the end, it is important to support it with subjective arguments. Rational weighing up will not help you in this situation.

There is no best alternative. Instead of looking for reasons out there, we should be looking for reasons in here. *Ruth Chang*

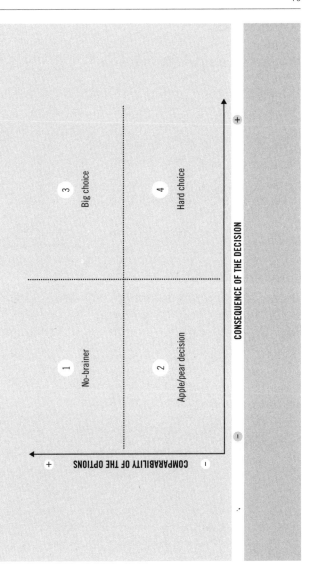

COMPARABILITY OF THE OPTIONS

CONSEQUENCE OF THE DECISION

1 No-brainer

2 Apple/pear decision

3 Big choice

4 Hard choice

COGNITIVE BIAS

THE FOUR MISTAKES WE MAKE IN OUR THINKING

	THE ANCHOR EFFECT	THE CONFIRMATION ERROR
ASSUMPTION	We considered all factors before making a decision.	We objectively assessed the situation before making a decision.
REALITY	We most strongly trust the very first information we are given: the first thing we hear about someone influences our judgement of the person; the first price we are quoted forms the basis for the negotiation. Thus the expression: 'You only get one chance for a first impression.' It takes a huge amount of persuasive power to hoist the anchor once it has been lowered.	We interpret information in such a way that it affirms our existing assumption or conviction. Or vice versa: we block out information that contradicts our opinions. Nobody googles counterarguments.
SOLUTION	Don't trust your first impressions.	Assume that you are wrong.

Cognitive biases are those systematic errors of judgement that we all make unconsciously and that influence our decisions. You can't eliminate these biases, but you can sharpen your thinking.

THE AVAILABILITY ERROR

We have good arguments for making a particular decision.

We base our arguments on simple, available and above all autobiographical information. You had a car accident with a Golf? VW makes awful cars! You once had a pretty girlfriend from Poland? All Polish people are good-looking!

Don't trust anecdotal evidence.

THE FAST/SLOW ERROR

We believe we have intuitively made the right decision.

Although impulsive decisions can be good (➥ see Theory of unconscious thinking, p. 44), they aren't always. Daniel Kahneman identified two styles of thinking: System 1 (quick and intuitive) and System 2 (slow and careful). An example: a coffee and a cookie together cost £1.10. The coffee costs £1 more than the cookie. How much does the cookie cost? Most people would immediately say 10 pence. This is the System 1 way of thinking. But if you think through the problem more carefully, i.e. with System 2, you will come to the right answer: the cookie costs 5 pence.

Read emails through again before sending them.

THE CROSSROADS MODEL

SO, WHAT NEXT?

We all have times in our lives when we find ourselves at a crossroads, and ask ourselves: Where now? The crossroads model helps you to find your direction in life. Fill in the model on the basis of the following questions:

Where have you come from?

How have you become who you are? What have been the main decisions, events and obstacles in your life, and who were your main influences? Think about your education, your home, where you grew up. And make a note of keywords that strike you as important.

What is really important to you?

Write down the first three things that come into your head. You don't have to go into detail or be specific. What are your values? What do you believe in? Which principles are important to you? When everything fails, what remains?

Which people are important to you?

Here you should think of people whose opinions you value, and who influence your decisions, as well as those who are affected by your decisions. Think also about the people you like and those you fear.

What is hindering you?

What aspects of your life prevent you from thinking about the really important things? Which deadlines do you have in your head, and what is hindering you? What do you have to do, and when?

What are you afraid of?

List the things, circumstances or people that cause you worry and rob you of your strength.

Look at your notes. What's missing? What issues have arisen? Do the keywords you've written down tell the story of how you became who you are today? If necessary, jot down more keywords and questions. Now look at the roads that lie ahead of you. We have given six examples. Imagine each one:

1. The road I have already been down.

2. The road that beckons – what have you always wanted to try?

3. The road that I imagine in my wildest dreams, regardless of whether it is achievable or not – what do you dream of?

4. The road that seems most sensible to me, the one that people whose opinion I value would suggest to me.

5. The road not travelled – one you have never considered before.

6. The road back to a place you once felt safe.

You decide.

When was the last time you did something for the first time?

The road back

The familiar road

The road not travelled

WHAT IS HINDERING YOU?

WHAT IS REALLY IMPORTANT TO YOU?

WHERE HAVE YO

Answer the questions by yourself or together with a good friend.
Then imagine the road that you could take.

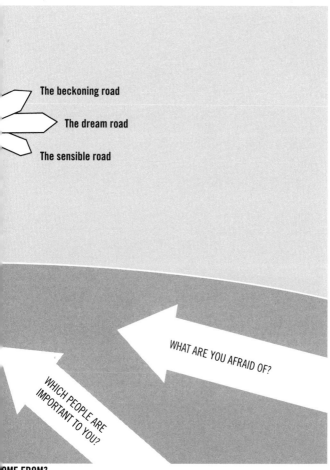

The beckoning road

The dream road

The sensible road

WHAT ARE YOU AFRAID OF?

WHICH PEOPLE ARE IMPORTANT TO YOU?

OME FROM?

HOW TO UNDERSTAND
OTHERS BETTER

THE RUMSFELD MATRIX

HOW TO ANALYSE RISKS MORE EFFECTIVELY

One of the more interesting risk analyses comes from a man who made massive misjudgements in risk analysis on several occasions. This man is Donald Rumsfeld, who was US Secretary of Defense under George W. Bush. For a press conference in 2002, he used a model to help him answer a journalist's question about whether Iraq was harbouring terrorists. He spoke of:

1. Knowns.

2. Unknowns.

These parameters result in four fields of risk:

1. Known knowns: These are risks that we know and against which we have developed countermeasures. For example, somebody who is afraid of thieves locks up their bike.

2. Known unknowns: These are risks that we know exist but cannot foresee. For example, we know that the stock market crashes occasionally, but nobody can precisely predict when or how far it will crash.

3. Unknown knowns: For example, scientists assume that there is part of us that knows more than we think we know. Whatever you call this part – intuition, inner voice, gut feeling – the following is important when it comes to decision-making: we are more likely to forgive mistakes made intuitively than mistakes that we spent a long time thinking about. In other words: we forgive our gut more than our brain.

4. Unknown unknowns: The things we don't know that we don't know. These are risks that we hadn't considered, because it did not even occur to us that they could exist. For example, when Pearl Harbor was attacked by Japanese kamikaze pilots in 1941, the USA wasn't prepared because it never would have imagined such an attack. And, according to Rumsfeld, it was an 'unforeseen' threat of this kind that the USA was dealing with in Iraq.

So what can we learn from this model? We advise against hiring Donald Rumsfeld as a risk analyst, but his conclusion offers food for thought: catastrophes that strike us unexpectedly reflect a lack of imagination.

Risk is what remains after we think we've thought of everything.

➥ See also: Black swan model (p. 112)

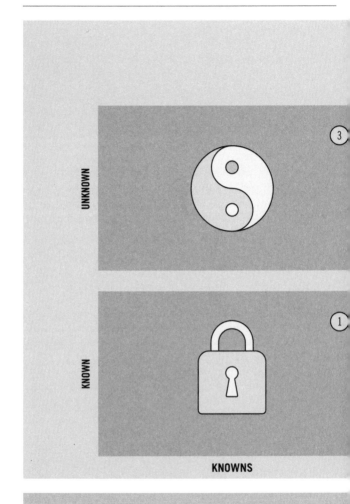

3

1

KNOWNS

'Unknown unknowns' (field 4): The Japanese attack on Pearl Harbor was an event that the USA had not reckoned on because it was simply unimaginable.

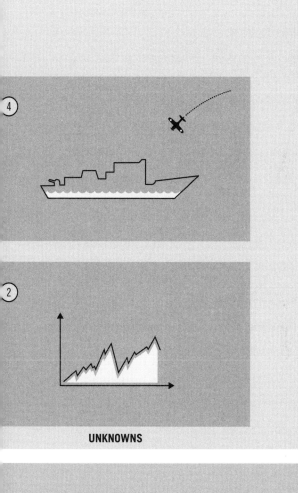

UNKNOWNS

THE SWISS CHEESE MODEL

HOW MISTAKES HAPPEN

Everyone makes mistakes. Some people learn from them, while others repeat them. Here is what you need to know about mistakes.

There are different types of mistake:

- real mistakes – occur when the wrong process is carried out

- black-outs – occur when part of a process is forgotten

- slip-ups – occur when the right process is carried out incorrectly

There are several levels on which mistakes occur:

- skill-based level

- rule-based level

- knowledge-based level

And there are various factors that contribute to mistakes occurring:

- people involved – boss, team, colleagues, friends

- technical provisions – equipment, workplace

- organisational elements – task to be fulfilled, timing

- outside influences – time, economic climate, mood, weather

The most impressive illustration of the causes and effects of mistakes is the human error or Swiss cheese model by James Reason (1990). The model compares the different levels on which mistakes occur with slices of Emmental cheese. In a mistake-free world, the cheese would have no holes. But in the real world, the cheese is cut into thin slices, and every slice has many holes, which are in different places in different slices. Imagine the holes as conduits for mistakes. A mistake remains unnoticed or irrelevant if it penetrates only one hole in one of the slices. But it can lead to catastrophe if the holes in the different slices align and the mistake passes through all the holes in all of the defences. The model is used in the fields of medicine and air traffic, for example – and anywhere where mistakes can have fatal consequences.

Experience is the name everyone gives to his mistakes. *Oscar Wilde*

➥ See also: Result optimisation model (p. 136)

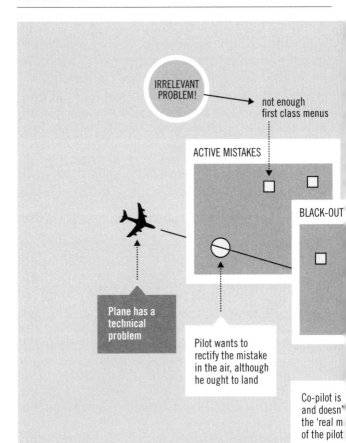

The illustration shows what happens when mistakes are made on three different levels, and three 'holes in the cheese' align:
1. The pilot makes a mistake. 2. The co-pilot reacts incorrectly.
3. While attempting to rectify the mistake, another is made.

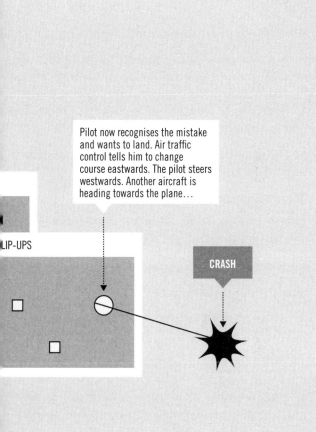

THE MASLOW PYRAMIDS

WHAT YOU ACTUALLY NEED, WHAT YOU ACTUALLY WANT

'The three most important questions,' begins the 2003 German film *Hierankl*, 'are: Are you having sex? Do you have a family? Are you intellectually stimulated? Scoring three yeses is paradise; two yeses is what you need to be happy, and one yes is what you need to survive.' The film is bad, but the questions it asks are good.

In 1943, the psychologist Abraham Maslow published a 'hierarchy of needs' model. He categorised human needs as follows:

- physiological needs (eating, sleeping, warmth, sex)

- security (somewhere to live, job security, health, protection against adversities)

- social relationships (friends, partner, love)

- recognition (status, power, money)

- self-actualisation (individuality, realising personal potential, but also faith and transcendence)

The first three of these are basic needs. If they are satisfied, a person no longer thinks about them. The last two are aspirations or personal growth needs; they can never really be satisfied. The pyramids model becomes interesting if we contrast our aspirations with our needs.

Rule of thumb for the Western world: the things we desire the most are the things we need the least.

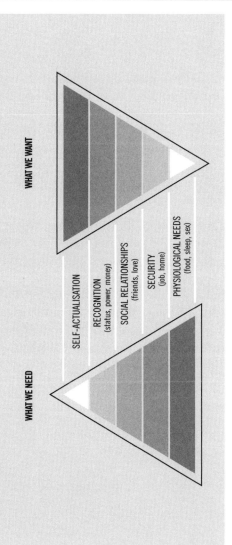

WHAT WE NEED — **WHAT WE WANT**

SELF-ACTUALISATION

RECOGNITION
(status, power, money)

SOCIAL RELATIONSHIPS
(friends, love)

SECURITY
(job, home)

PHYSIOLOGICAL NEEDS
(food, sleep, sex)

Create your own personal basic needs pyramids. What do you have? What do you want?

THE SINUS MILIEU AND BOURDIEU MODELS

WHERE YOU BELONG

The Sinus Milieu is a psychographic method for establishing the different socio-cultural groupings to which a person belongs. It is often used in marketing to define target groups. The idea was developed by the French sociologist Émile Durkheim. On the next double page is a rarely used version by another French sociologist, Pierre Bourdieu, in the form of an axis model. Bourdieu's analysis of cultural consumption challenges us to think about our deep-rooted cultural preferences and practices.

The narrowness of the Sinus groups is often criticised. It is true that it cannot answer the question 'Where do I belong if my father was a bus driver, my mother a hippy, I am a fashion designer and in my spare time I hang out with my friends from the golf club?' The popularity of such models (the other big player is the Limbic® Types by Nymphenburg) can be explained by the lock-in principle: almost all market research and market analyses are concerned with segmentation. It shows us that if a majority have become used to one system, it is difficult for another system to establish itself. Habit is stronger than the desire for improvement.

Our origins are our future. *Martin Heidegger*

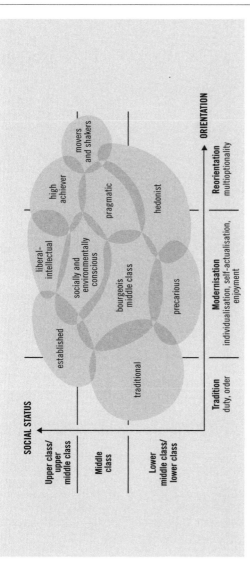

Sinus Milieu model: Where would you position yourself? Where would you position your parents? Where would you like to be positioned?

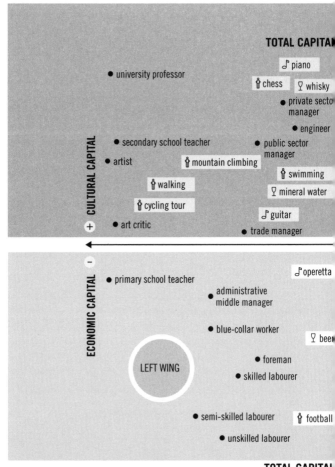

Bourdieu model: Where would you position yourself?
Where would you position your parents?
And where would you like to be positioned?

(cultural and economic)

♟ golf ♟ bridge

♟ tennis ♟ water skiing

• industry businessman

• trade businessman

♟ Scrabble

♟ sailing

RIGHT WING

♟ riding

♀ champagne

♟ hunting

— CULTURAL CAPITAL

+ ECONOMIC CAPITAL

• small businessman

• tradesman

♟ pétanque

♀ sparkling wine

♟ fishing

• farmer

♪ accordion

♀ table wine

• farm-worker

(cultural and economic)

THE DOUBLE-LOOP LEARNING MODEL

HOW TO LEARN FROM YOUR MISTAKES

Double-loop learning involves reflecting on your actions and learning from them. It sounds simple but is almost impossible.

The theory is based on the work of the system theoreticians Heinz von Foerster and Niklas Luhmann, in particular on the idea of 'second-order observation'. Strictly speaking, this is not a model but a technique for know-alls. How can you master this desirable technique? Simple: you learn how to observe first-order observers.

First-order observers see things as they appear to them. For them, the world is simply there. Second-order observers, on the other hand, attribute *what* the first-order observers see to *how* they see it. In other words, second-order observers observe a way of observing. During the act of observing, first-order observers are unaware of their own way of observing – it is their blind spot. Recognising this blind spot enables second-order observers to become know-alls. They are able to point out to the first-order observers that it is possible to observe differently and thus see things differently.

The psychologist Chris Argyris and the philosopher Donald Schön developed double-loop learning out of these theoretical ideas on observation. In the best-case scenario, the single loop (the first-order observation) is best practice. Something that works well is not changed but simply repeated. In the worst-case scenario it is worst practice – the same mistake is repeated, or a problem is solved without questioning how it arose in the first place.

In double-loop learning you think about and question what you are doing, and try to break your own pattern, not simply by doing something differently, but by thinking about why you do it the way you do it. What are the objectives and values behind your actions? If you are fully aware of these, you may be able to change them.

The problem inherent in the double loop is the discrepancy between what we say we are about to do (known as espoused theory) and what we actually do (known as theory in use). If we really want to change something, it is not enough to create guidelines for our employees or ourselves, or to give directives. These only reach us as a command (espoused theory). Real changes occur when we reassess our more deeply rooted reasons, objectives and values. These are the 'force fields' that affect the theory in use.

We deserve what we have. As long as we don't change it.

➥ See also: Black box model (p. 118)

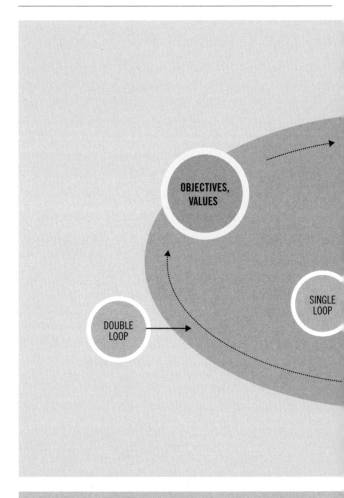

When was the last time you broke a familiar pattern in your life and really did something differently? Which pattern would you like to break? What is preventing you from breaking it?

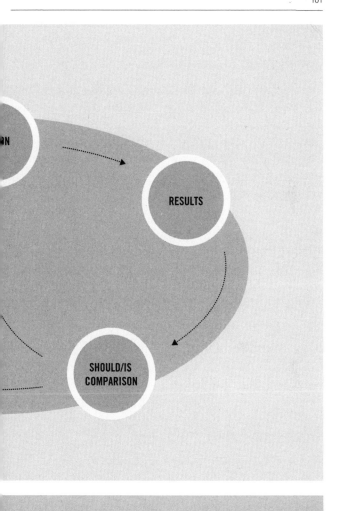

THE AI MODEL

WHAT KIND OF DISCUSSION TYPE ARE YOU?

The abbreviation AI stands for Appreciative Inquiry, a method attributed to the American management expert David Cooperrider that involves concentrating on the strengths, positive attributes and potential of a company or a person, rather than weaknesses. 'What is going really well at the moment?' replaces the classic question 'What is the problem?' Concentrating on weakness creates a negative impression from the outset.

Every person, every system, every product, every idea has faults. In the best-case scenario, an awareness of this fact can lead to a determined pursuit of perfection. But in many cases, focusing too strongly on the flaws of an idea or project stifles the open and positive approach that is essential for good working practices. The basic principle is to take an idea that is not yet fully developed and to continue developing it, instead of prematurely abandoning it.

People often reveal their character in their approach to discussions. Depending on how they react to suggestions, they fall into one of the following four categories:

- **The fault-finder:** 'The idea is good, but ...'

- **The dictator:** 'No!'

- **The schoolteacher:** 'No, the idea isn't good because ...'

- **The AI thinker:** 'Yes, and we could also ...'

Any fool can criticise. And most fools do. *Benjamin Franklin*

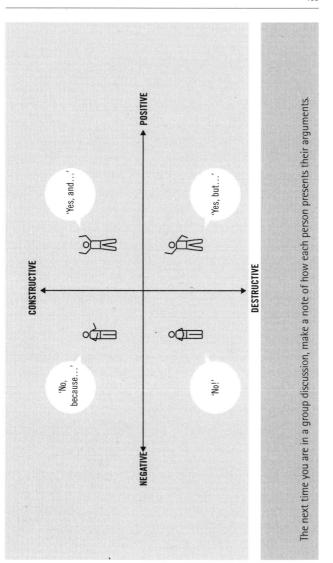

The next time you are in a group discussion, make a note of how each person presents their arguments.

THE PARETO PRINCIPLE

WHY 80 PER CENT OF THE OUTPUT IS ACHIEVED WITH
20 PER CENT OF THE INPUT

At the beginning of the twentieth century, the Italian economist Vilfredo Pareto observed that 80 per cent of Italy's wealth belonged to 20 per cent of the population. And that's not all: 20 per cent of workers do 80 per cent of the work; 20 per cent of criminals commit 80 per cent of the crimes. Today we know that 20 per cent of car drivers cause 80 per cent of accidents. And 20 per cent of hedge funds invest 80 per cent of the money invested; 20 per cent of pubgoers consume 80 per cent of the alcohol consumed. We wear 20 per cent of the clothes we have in our wardrobes and spend 80 per cent of our time with 20 per cent of our friends. In business meetings, 80 per cent of the decisions are made in 20 per cent of the time, and 20 per cent of a company's clients (products) are responsible for 80 per cent of its turnover.

Of course, the Pareto rule cannot be applied to everything (mathematicians prefer the more precise '64/4' rule, because 80 per cent of 80 is 64 and 20 per cent of 20 is 4). But anybody who wants to plan their time optimally should know that roughly 20 per cent of the time spent on a task leads to 80 per cent of the results.

I am definitely going to take a course on time management … just as soon as I can work it into my schedule. *Louis E. Boone*

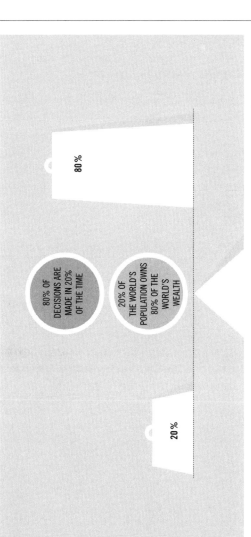

The Pareto principle describes the statistical phenomenon whereby a small number of high values contribute more to the total than a high number of low values.

80%

80% OF DECISIONS ARE MADE IN 20% OF THE TIME

20% OF THE WORLD'S POPULATION OWNS 80% OF THE WORLD'S WEALTH

20%

THE LONG-TAIL MODEL

HOW THE INTERNET IS TRANSFORMING THE ECONOMY

Forget everything you just read about the 'Pareto Principle' – the idea that 20 per cent of products generate 80 per cent of turnover. In 2004, the editor-in-chief of *Wired*, Chris Anderson, claimed that nearly everything that is offered for sale on the internet is also actually sold – however bizarre or unnecessary the product. As a result, business gravitates to where there is variety instead of uniformity.

Anderson used a demand curve to illustrate his claim. On the far left, the curve rises sharply upwards. Here are the best-sellers and block-busters that account for 20 per cent of the market. Then the curve levels out gently to the right. This is where we find the less popular books and films. This part of the curve is much wider, spanning many more products, than the peak. Instinctively one would think the Pareto principle is right: the best-sellers (20 per cent) are more profitable than the 'rest-sellers' (80 per cent). But the figures suggest something different: the long tail achieves a higher turnover than the few best-sellers. In 2004, this was a bold theory. Nowadays it is standard in many industries.

The internet is the world's largest library. It's just that all the books are on the floor. *John Allen Paulos*

➥ See also: Pareto principle (p. 104)

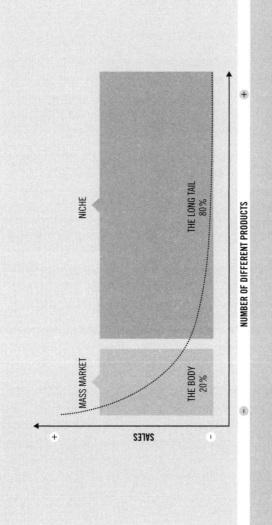

SALES

NUMBER OF DIFFERENT PRODUCTS

MASS MARKET

NICHE

THE BODY
20%

THE LONG TAIL
80%

The mass market wants best-sellers, but there is also a demand for niche products. Individual demand may be low, but collectively the niche products are worth more than the best-sellers.

THE CONFLICT RESOLUTION MODEL

HOW TO RESOLVE A CONFLICT ELEGANTLY

Psychologists agree that conflicts have to be dealt with in order to prevent deadlock and recrimination and restore stability and communication. The question is, how? In principle there are six different ways of dealing with a conflict situation: escape, fight, give up, evade responsibility, compromise or reach a consensus.

1. **Flight.** Escaping is the same as avoiding. The conflict is not dealt with, and the situation remains the same. It can be assumed that neither side will gain anything. This is a lose–lose situation.

2. **Fight.** Those who deal with a conflict aggressively have only one aim: to win. But winning alone is not enough, as somebody also has to lose. This approach is about conquering the opponent, and asserting one's own position in the face of resistance from others. The result is a win–lose situation.

3. **Give up.** Those who give up their own position in a conflict solve it by retreating, i.e. they lose. The result is a lose–win situation.

4. **Evade responsibility.** Those who feel overwhelmed by a conflict often delegate the decision – and thus also the confrontation – to another authority, usually a higher one. This authority solves the conflict for them, but not necessarily wisely, and not necessarily in the delegator's interest. There is a risk that the parties on both sides of the conflict will lose (lose–lose situation).

5. **Compromise.** Depending on how it is perceived, a compromise is a solution acceptable to both parties. It is often felt that although the solution isn't ideal, it is reasonable in the circumstances (win-lose/win-lose).

6. **Reach a consensus.** A consensus is based on a new solution that has been developed by both parties. In contrast to a compromise, it is a win-win situation for both parties, because nobody has to back down. Instead, both parties develop a 'third way' together.

Our failures are due not to the defeats we suffer but to the conflicts we don't participate in. *Graffiti on a youth centre in Bern, Switzerland*

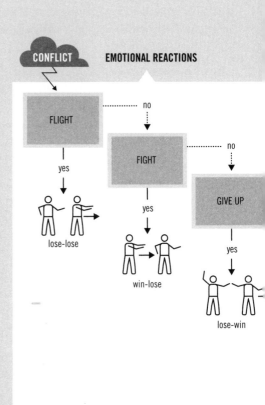

This model shows the six typical reactions to a conflict.
What conflict type are you? What type is your adversary?

RATIONAL REACTIONS

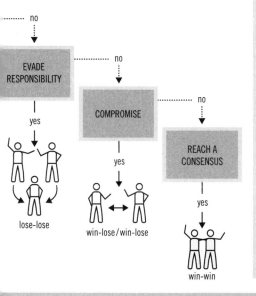

no

EVADE RESPONSIBILITY

yes

lose-lose

no

COMPROMISE

yes

win-lose / win-lose

no

REACH A CONSENSUS

yes

win-win

THE BLACK SWAN MODEL

WHY YOUR EXPERIENCES DON'T MAKE YOU ANY WISER

Here are three questions for a reflective person: How do we know what we know? Does the past help us predict the future? Why do we never expect unexpected events?

In his 1912 book *The Problems of Philosophy*, Bertrand Russell summarised the answers to all three questions: a chicken that expects to be fed every day assumes that it will continue to be fed every day. It starts to firmly believe that humans are kind. Nothing in the chicken's life points to the fact that one day it will be slaughtered.

We humans also have to acknowledge that the biggest catastrophes usually come as a complete surprise to us. That's why, according to Russell, we should always question the things we take for granted.

For example, when two Boeing airliners were flown into the World Trade Center, the public was shocked – the catastrophe seemed to strike completely without warning. However, in the weeks and months following 11 September 2001, it seemed that practically everything had pointed towards this attack.

The Lebanese writer Nassim Nicholas Taleb calls this phenomenon – our inability to predict the future from the past – the black swan. In the Western world it was always assumed that all swans were white – until naturalists in the seventeenth century discovered a breed of black swans. What had hitherto been unimaginable was suddenly taken for granted.

Taleb's black swan thesis is not really a model, but a rejection of the cause-and-effect principle. And it reminds us that we tend to cling most tightly to pillars that we see toppling.

What were the black swans – the unexpected events – in your life, and when did they occur?

➥ See also: Rumsfeld matrix (p. 84), Black box model (p. 118)

THE CHASM – THE DIFFUSION MODEL

WHY EVERYBODY HAD AN iPOD

Why is it that some ideas – including stupid ones – take hold and become trends, while others bloom briefly before withering and disappearing from the public eye?

The sociologist Everett Rogers described the way in which a catchy idea or product becomes popular as 'diffusion'. One of the most famous diffusion studies is an analysis by Bruce Ryan and Neal Gross of the diffusion of hybrid corn in the 1930s in Greene County, Iowa. The new type of corn was better than the old sort in every way, yet it took twenty-two years for it to become widely accepted.

The diffusion researchers called the farmers who switched to the new corn as early as 1928 'innovators', and the somewhat bigger group that was infected by them 'early adopters'. They were the opinion leaders in the communities, respected people who observed the experiments of the innovators and then joined them. They were followed at the end of the 1930s by the 'sceptical masses', those who would never change anything before it had been tried out by the successful farmers. But at some point even they were infected by the 'hybrid corn virus', and eventually transmitted it to the die-hard conservatives, the 'stragglers'.

Translated into a graph, this development takes the form of a curve typical of the progress of an epidemic. It rises, gradually at first, then reaches the critical point of any newly launched product, when many products fail. The critical point for any innovation is the transition from the early adopters to the sceptics, for at this point there is a 'chasm'. According to the US sociologist Morton Grodzins, if the early adopters succeed in getting the innovation across the chasm to the sceptical masses, the epidemic cycle reaches the tipping point. From there, the curve rises sharply when the masses accept the product, and sinks again when only the stragglers remain.

First they ignore you, then they laugh at you, then they fight you, then you win. *Mahatma Gandhi*

➥ See also: Pareto principle (p. 104), Long-tail model (p. 106)

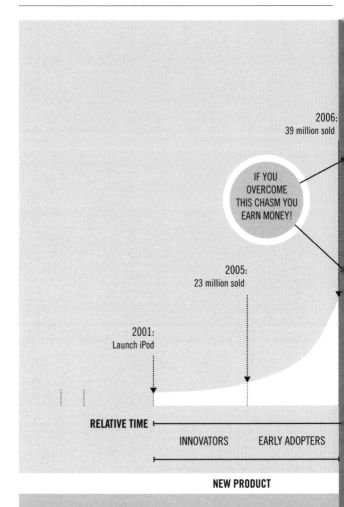

The model shows the typical curve of a product launch, based on
the example of the iPod.

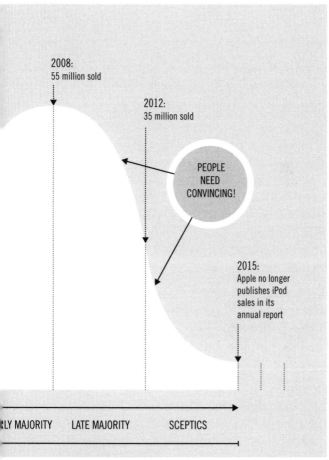

2008:
55 million sold

2012:
35 million sold

PEOPLE
NEED
CONVINCING!

2015:
Apple no longer
publishes iPod
sales in its
annual report

RLY MAJORITY   LATE MAJORITY   SCEPTICS

ESTABLISHED PRODUCT

THE BLACK BOX MODEL

WHY FAITH IS REPLACING KNOWLEDGE

One thing is undisputed: our world is getting more complicated all the time. Black and white, good and bad, right and wrong have been displaced by complicated constructs that leave most people in the dark.

As the world around us becomes increasingly fast-paced and complex, the amount that we really know – that we can really grasp and understand – decreases all the time. As recently as the 1980s, teachers still tried to explain to their pupils how computers worked in terms of binary code. Today it is more or less taken for granted that we do not understand many of the things that surround us and that we use, e.g. smartphones. And even if somebody tried to explain the DNA code to us, we would probably be out of our depth.

We are increasingly surrounded by 'black boxes', complex constructs that we do not understand even if they are explained to us. We cannot comprehend the inner processes of a black box, but none the less we integrate their inputs and outputs into our decision-making.

The amount that we simply *have* to believe, without understanding it, is increasing all the time. As a result, we tend to assign more importance to those who can explain something than to their actual explanation.

In the future it will be the norm to convince people with images and emotions rather than with arguments.

➼ See also: Black swan model (p. 112)

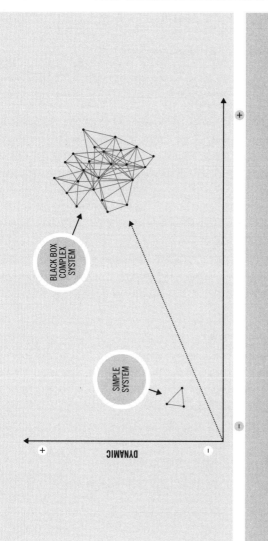

The speed and complexity of a process increase in relation to each other. We are often no longer able to understand increasingly complex explanations.

THE PRISONER'S DILEMMA

WHEN IS IT WORTH TRUSTING SOMEONE?

As the saying goes, 'Trust makes way for treachery'. But is this true? Here's a puzzle that provides an answer.

Two prisoners are suspected of having carried out a crime together. The maximum sentence for the crime is ten years. The two suspects have been arrested separately, and each is offered the same deal: if he confesses that they both committed the crime and his accomplice remains silent, the charges against him will be dropped – but his accomplice will have to serve the full ten years. If both he and his accomplice remain silent, there will only be circumstantial evidence, which will none the less be enough to put both men behind bars for two years. But if both he and his accomplice confess to the crime, they will both be sentenced to five years in prison. The suspects cannot confer. How should they react under questioning? Should they trust each other?

This is the so-called prisoner's dilemma, a classic conundrum in game theory. The two suspects both lose if they opt for the most obvious solution – i.e. to put themselves first: they get a five-year sentence each. They fare better if each one trusts that the other will remain silent: they then get a two-year sentence each. Note that if only one of the suspects confesses, then the sentence is ten years for the other suspect and the confessor is freed.

In 1979 the political scientist Robert Axelrod organised a tournament in which fourteen academic colleagues played 200 rounds of the prisoner's dilemma against one another in order to work out the best strategy. He found that in the first round it is best to cooperate with your accomplice (i.e. trust him). In the second round, do what your accomplice did in the previous round. By imitating his moves, he will follow yours.

You can't shake hands with a clenched fist. *Indira Gandhi*

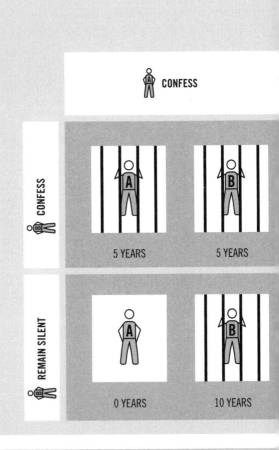

You and your accomplice are on trial. If only you confess, your accomplice will serve ten years. If you both remain silent, you will both serve two years. If both of you confess, you will both serve five years. You cannot confer. How should you react?

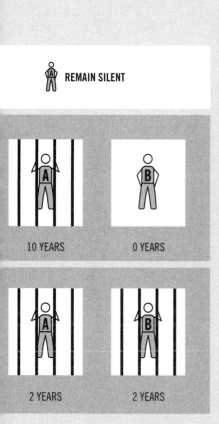

REMAIN SILENT

10 YEARS

0 YEARS

2 YEARS

2 YEARS

HOW TO IMPROVE OTHERS

THE TEAM MODEL

IS YOUR TEAM UP TO THE JOB?

Regardless of whether you are the head of a kindergarten or of a national sports team, or whether you want to set up a company or a fundraising committee, you will be asking yourself the same questions: Do I have the right people for this project? Do our skills correspond to our goals? Are we capable of doing what we want to do?

This team model will help you to judge your team. Begin by defining the skills, expertise and resources that you think are important for carrying out the project. Note the skills that are absolutely necessary for the job. Distinguish between soft skills (e.g. loyalty, motivation, reliability) and hard skills (e.g. computer, business and knowledge of foreign languages). For each skill, define where your critical boundary lies on a scale of zero to ten. For example, an acceptable level of fluency in French might be five. Now judge your 'players' according to these criteria. Connect the points with a line. What are the team's weaknesses, and what are their strengths?

Even more revealing than the model itself is the subsequent self-evaluation by the team members. A good team is one that can correctly judge its own capabilities.

Beware! Real strength lies in differences, not in similarities.

The best executive is the one who has sense enough to pick good men to do what he wants done, and self-restraint enough to keep from meddling with them while they do it. Theodore Roosevelt

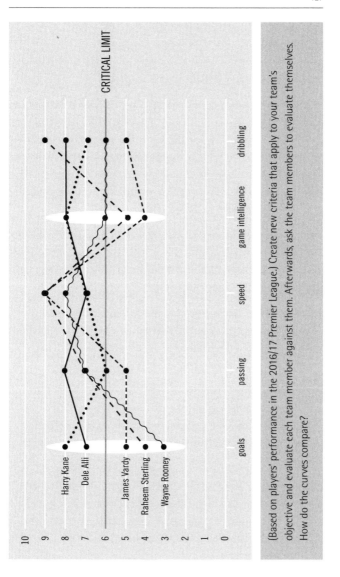

(Based on players' performance in the 2016/17 Premier League.) Create new criteria that apply to your team's objective and evaluate each team member against them. Afterwards, ask the team members to evaluate themselves. How do the curves compare?

THE HERSEY–BLANCHARD MODEL (SITUATIONAL LEADERSHIP)

HOW TO SUCCESSFULLY MANAGE YOUR EMPLOYEES

Over the last hundred years, organisational theory has taken many different turns. Man is a machine and should be treated as such (Taylor, Ford). Paying attention to social factors, and not objectively regulated working conditions, leads to the best results (Hawthorne). Organisations can regulate themselves (Clark, Farley). And strategic management, i.e. the division of organisations into primary and secondary activities, leads to success (Porter).

A rather different theory was put forward by Paul Hersey and Ken Blanchard, who suggested that the most important thing is to adapt one's style of leadership to the situation at hand. This 'situational leadership model' distinguishes between:

1. **Instructing.** When they are starting a job, employees need strong leadership. When they are new their level of commitment is usually high, but their level of expertise is still low. Employees are given orders and instructions.

2. **Coaching.** The employees' level of expertise has risen. Because of stress and the loss of the initial euphoria at starting a new job, their motivation and commitment levels have fallen. The employees are asked questions, and they look for the answers themselves.

3. **Supporting.** The level of expertise has risen sharply. The level of motivation can vary: either it has gone down (employees may resign) or it has gone up as a result of being given more independence (employees are encouraged to come up with their own ideas).

4. Delegating. Employees are fully in control of their work. The level of motivation is high. They are given their own projects and lead their own teams.

Lead your employees in such a way that you yourself become superfluous. And lead your employees to be successful, so that one day they will be in a leadership position themselves.

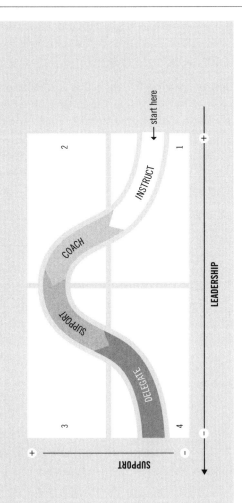

Read from right to left. New employees must first be instructed, then coached, then supported, and finally delegated to.

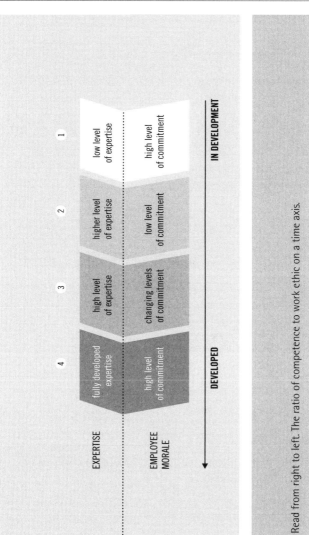

	4	3	2	1
EXPERTISE	fully developed expertise	high level of expertise	higher level of expertise	low level of expertise
EMPLOYEE MORALE	high level of commitment	changing levels of commitment	low level of commitment	high level of commitment

DEVELOPED ←→ IN DEVELOPMENT

Read from right to left. The ratio of competence to work ethic on a time axis.

THE ROLE-PLAYING MODEL (BELBIN & DE BONO)

HOW TO CHANGE YOUR OWN POINT OF VIEW

When the creative-thinking guru Edward de Bono presented his 'six thinking hats' in 1986, critics dismissed the idea as just a bit of fun. De Bono's idea was to assign the members of a working group a temporary one-dimensional point of view or 'thinking hat'. Today, the technique is widely accepted, and De Bono's six hats are used as a team or meeting technique to stimulate communication and create a playful/serious approach to a discussion topic.

This is how it works. An idea or a strategy is discussed by the members of a group. During the discussion, all the members adopt one of the six points of view – reflected in the colour of the hat. (It is important that all members of the group wear the same colour hat at the same time.)

- **White hat:** analytical, objective thinking, the emphasis is on facts and feasibility.

- **Red hat:** emotional thinking, subjective feelings, perceptions and opinions.

- **Black hat:** critical thinking, risk assessment, identifying problems, scepticism, critique.

- **Yellow hat:** optimistic thinking, speculative best-case scenario.

- **Green hat:** creative, associative thinking, new ideas, brainstorming, constructive.

- **Blue hat:** structured thinking, process overview, the big picture.

Beware! The meeting must be moderated to ensure that the team members do not slip out of their designated role.

Homogenous teams, i.e. teams in which the members have similar views and character traits, don't work as well. In the 1970s, Meredith Belbin studied individuals and character roles and their influence on group processes. Based on his observations, he identified nine different profiles:

- **Action-oriented:** doer, implementer, perfectionist.

- **Communication-oriented:** coordinator, team player, trailblazer.

- **Knowledge-oriented:** innovator, observer, specialist.

If you have a good idea, but fear that it may meet with strong resistance, try to lead the discussion in such a way that the other members of the group think that they came up with the idea themselves. The more that people feel they have generated an idea themselves, the more passionately they fight for its implementation. If nobody claims to have come up with the idea, perhaps it wasn't that good in the first place!

I never did anything alone. What was accomplished, was accomplished collectively. *Golda Meir*

➥ See also: Drexler/Sibbet team performance model® (p. 140)

TEAM ROLE	CONTRIBUTION
The plant	introduces new ideas
Resource investigator	investigates possibilities, develops contacts
Coordinator	encourages decision-making processes, delegates
Shaper	overcomes obstacles
Monitor	examines feasibility
Team worker	improves communication, gets things moving
Implementor	puts ideas into practice
Completer	conscientious, prompt
Specialist	provides specialist knowledge

In the 1970s, Meredith Belbin investigated different personality types in terms of their team performance. He identified nine different types of team player.

CHARACTER	PERMISSIBLE WEAKNESS
unorthodox thinking	absent-minded
communicative, extrovert	over-optimistic
independent, responsible	appears manipulative
dynamic, works well under pressure	impatient, provocative
level-headed, strategic, critical	uninspired
cooperative, diplomatic	indecisive
disciplined, reliable, effective	inflexible
ensures optimal results	timid, hardly delegates
self-reliant, committed	gets lost in the details

THE RESULT OPTIMISATION MODEL

WHY THE PRINTER ALWAYS BREAKS DOWN JUST BEFORE A DEADLINE

There are many project management models and methods. Most of them are based on the premise that there is a fixed amount of time in which to carry out a project. Generally, within this time, ideas are gathered (G) and consolidated (C), and a concept is selected and implemented (I). In real life, we all know that we never have enough time. And the little time we do have is reduced by unforeseen events like a printer breaking down just when you want to use it.

The result optimisation model divides the available time into three sequences (loops) of equal length, thereby forcing the project manager to complete the project three times. The idea is to improve the outcome in each successive working loop. This method leads not only to improved output quality but also to a more successful final outcome: at the end of a project, instead of simply being glad that it is 'finally put to bed', the whole team's sense of achievement is intensified threefold.

Beware! Be stringent when carrying out this strategy: work in such a way that each loop is properly completed before embarking on the next. Otherwise this model loses its dynamic.

With development processes, it is important to clearly separate the three stages, those of gathering, consolidation and implementation.

A beautiful thing is never perfect. *Anonymous*

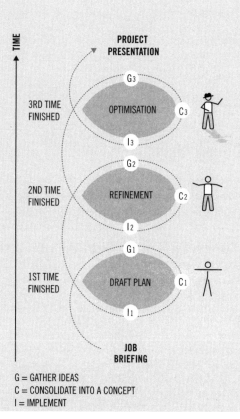

G = GATHER IDEAS
C = CONSOLIDATE INTO A CONCEPT
I = IMPLEMENT

To achieve an optimal result, you should plan your project so that it is 'finished' three times. After the third time it really is finished.

THE PROJECT MANAGEMENT TRIANGLE

WHY PERFECTION IS IMPOSSIBLE

Good, cheap or fast – these are the three success factors governing the service industry. The *or* is important, because usually it is only possible to offer two of the three:

- Good and fast is expensive.

- Fast and cheap is bad.

- Good and cheap is slow.

When you manage a project – whether a business idea, a dinner party or a Master's thesis – the same three success criteria apply: objective (what do I want to achieve, and in what quality?), duration (what is my time frame?), expenditure (what is the maximum I can spend in terms of money or resources?). But beware: the reality rarely lives up to the plan. Perhaps the project needs to be completed faster – then you need more resources. Or it needs to be cheaper – then the quality will suffer. Or you want to improve the quality – then you need more time.

Nothing is less productive than doing what should not be done at all. *Peter F. Drucker*

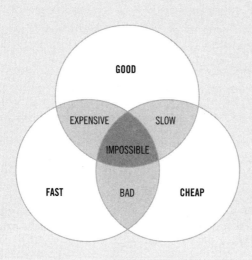

Good, fast, cheap – you can only have two.

THE DREXLER/SIBBET TEAM PERFORMANCE MODEL®

HOW TO TURN A GROUP INTO A TEAM

There are hundreds of team performance models and strategies out there. One of the best was developed by Allan Drexler, founder of the consulting company Drexler & Associates, and David Sibbet, founders of consulting company The Grove Consultants International. The model illustrates seven different stages that participants in a project typically go through.

Follow the arrows. At every stage there is a basic question that we ask ourselves at that point in a project (at the beginning: 'Why am I here?'; in the middle: 'How will we do it?'; at the end: 'Why continue?'), and 'keys', which describe team-members' behaviours, and which in turn indicate whether that particular stage has been resolved or not. The keys describe the feelings that we have when we are struggling with a particular stage, as well as the feelings we have once that stage has been successfully completed. For example, 'Goal Clarification' is resolved when team members display a shared vision. It may be unresolved if team members show apathy and scepticism, and if so this stage should be revisited. Many of the stages may seem obvious and trivial, but experience shows that every team goes through every stage. If a team skips a stage, it will end up returning to it later.

If you are leading a team, you should present the team model at the beginning of the project. After the project has started, ask the members of your team at regular intervals:

- How far along (i.e. at which stage of the project) are you?

- What do you need to do to reach the next stage?

If you are unsure about which stage your team is currently at, write down some 'keys' for each respective stage (see illustration), and ask: 'Which ones apply to you personally? Which ones apply to you as a team?'

Don't be afraid of stirring up negative feelings among the group. An open conflict is better than one that simmers unresolved through several stages and forces you to address issues during the final stages that should have been dealt with much earlier on.

Beware! Don't try to align your team rigidly to the model. The model is simply an aid to orientation: it is a compass, not a pacemaker.

Groups move forward only when one of the participants dares to take the first step. As leader, you should be prepared to be the first to make mistakes.

➥ See also: Role-playing model (p. 132)

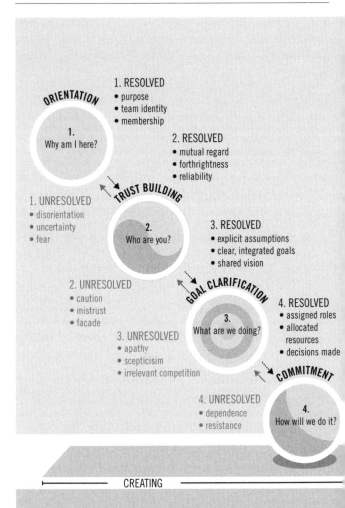

ORIENTATION

1. RESOLVED
- purpose
- team identity
- membership

1.
Why am I here?

2. RESOLVED
- mutual regard
- forthrightness
- reliability

1. UNRESOLVED
- disorientation
- uncertainty
- fear

TRUST BUILDING

2.
Who are you?

3. RESOLVED
- explicit assumptions
- clear, integrated goals
- shared vision

2. UNRESOLVED
- caution
- mistrust
- facade

GOAL CLARIFICATION

3.
What are we doing?

4. RESOLVED
- assigned roles
- allocated resources
- decisions made

3. UNRESOLVED
- apathy
- scepticisim
- irrelevant competition

COMMITMENT

4. UNRESOLVED
- dependence
- resistance

4.
How will we do it?

CREATING

The team performance model shows the seven stages that every
group goes through when carrying out a project.

7. RESOLVED
• recognition and celebration
• change mastery
• staying power

RENEWAL

7.
Why continue?

7. UNRESOLVED
• boredom
• burnout

6. RESOLVED
• spontaneous interaction
• synergy
• surpassing results

HIGH PERFORMANCE

6.
Wow!

6. UNRESOLVED
• overload
• disharmony

RESOLVED
lear processes
lignment
isciplined
xecution

IMPLEMENTATION

5.
Who does what, when, where?

5. UNRESOLVED
• conflict/confusion
• non-alignment
• missed deadlines

SUSTAINING

THE EXPECTATIONS MODEL

WHAT TO CONSIDER WHEN CHOOSING A PARTNER

Our little model illustrates the problem of high expectations based on the example of choosing a partner. If you have no expectations of your future partner, then you are indifferent – and indifferent decisions are rarely satisfying. The higher your expectations, the happier you are when you find a partner that lives up to them. You could say that having expectations increases our overall feeling of happiness. But there is a tipping point: if your expectations exceed a critical point, disappointment is inevitable, because whatever you are dreaming of becomes unattainable. Experience teaches us that perfection is a bit like the Loch Ness Monster: there are people who search for it their whole life – but nobody has ever seen it.

Of course, in principle there is nothing wrong with having high expectations. But if you have the feeling that your standards can never be met, ask yourself: What would you lose if you lowered your expectations?

Better a diamond with a flaw than a pebble without. *Confucius*

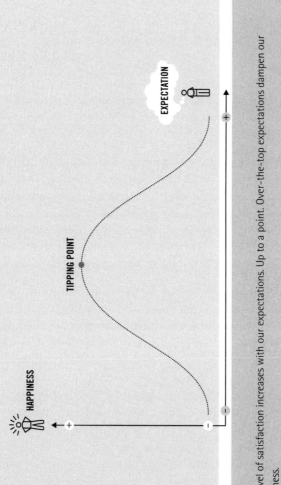

HAPPINESS

TIPPING POINT

EXPECTATION

Our level of satisfaction increases with our expectations. Up to a point. Over-the-top expectations dampen our happiness.

HOW WILL WE DECIDE IN THE FUTURE?

By Karin Frick
Head of Research, Gottlieb Duttweiler Institute

Almost ten years ago I wrote an essay for the first edition of this book about models of the future. Now I have been asked to check my essay to see if my prognoses were correct – or if they missed the mark (we actually don't review our prognoses often enough ➥ see Feedback analysis, p. 20)

The gist of my argument at the time was that interconnectivity was the new causality. We didn't need (decision-making) models any-more. Causal connections, I argued, were becoming less important, because intelligent machines make deductions based on data not models. Almost everything that we do, buy and decide nowadays, I wrote, leaves behind digital traces that will be gathered, analysed and used.

And it is true that leaving a 'digital footprint' is now the norm. The data scientists at Google, Facebook and Netflix know more about the behaviour and desires of their users than all social, consumer psychology and marketing experts – who rely on socio-scientific theories and models – combined. The most powerful management tools of the coming years will not be intelligent analyses but intelligent assistants. Siri and Amazon Echo will soon know us better than we know ourselves, Google's artificial intelligence already suggests goals for the coming year of its own accord. And it is absolutely undisputed that AI and smart assistants are revolutionising our decision-making behaviour and will show us new ways of looking at, understanding and organising the world. These 'intelligent agents' will change our view of the world as drastically as the telescope changed the way we look at the sky. In concrete terms, two things become possible:

1. AI will view reality from many different perspectives and therefore more objectively.

2. AI will be able to take into account different information in real time in its analyses – unlike humans, who work with subjective experiences from the past.

How does this change decisions made by managers?

The model on the following page was developed by the IT expert Andrew McAfee. When decisions are made based on a limited amount of data – as is still often the case today – the opinion of the most important person in the room traditionally holds sway. Generally, this person is also the highest-paid. McAfee calls it HiPPO: Highest Paid Person's Opinion. The underlying logic is that the person is well paid not because she makes such great decisions, but because she bears the ultimate responsibility. But the more data that flows into the decision-making process, the better (potentially) are the decisions we make, and the more irrelevant the HiPPOs become. Data becomes a tool for breaking down hierarchies.

So can we look forward to a better, brighter future?

In the future, decision-makers will work with AI-controlled prognosis tools rather than with models. There is an opportunity here: these tools are free of cognitive bias (unlike humans, ➥ see Cognitive bias, p. 76). But there is also a problem: we do not understand what these machines are calculating and, above all, what values their decisions are based on. The algorithms that rule the world are black boxes, understood by only a few experts. And these new aids to thinking may create their own reality.

'We have developed speed, but we have shut ourselves in. Machinery that gives abundance has left us in want. Our knowledge has made us cynical. Our cleverness, hard and unkind. We think too much and feel too little. More than machinery we need humanity. More than cleverness we need kindness and gentleness. Without these qualities, life will be violent and all will be lost.' These words, spoken by Charlie Chaplin in *The Great Dictator* almost eighty years ago, are still alarmingly relevant. In essence, they express the following: we should welcome progress and development, but be wary of how it is put to use.

Alongside moral and philosophical issues, there are practical ones, too. We are currently experiencing the paradox of plenty: huge amounts of data result in incredible precision but simultaneously in great confusion. The volume, speed and diversity of the data inevitably lead to patterns and connections being found – but these patterns and connections don't necessarily create meaning.

Ten years ago I came to the conclusion that the models in this book are not to be underestimated. Because even if they are old and analogue, they still help us to focus on what is important in an increasingly confusing and chaotic world; to think about values and remain responsible for our actions – something that we don't want to delegate to machines. Today, in the age of thinking machines and DAOs (Decentralised Autonomous Organisations), I believe this more than ever before.

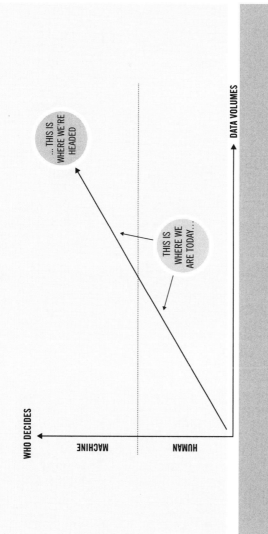

NOW IT'S YOUR TURN

DRAWING LESSON

WHY YOU SHOULD DRAW WHILE YOU TALK

- **Draw while you talk.** When they are drawn in real time, even imprecise or arbitrary elements are understood by the viewer – and treated more leniently.

- **Pictures say more than a thousand words.** Draw an iceberg to draw attention to a growing problem, a temple if you want to illustrate pillars of success, a bridge to show connections, rough outlines of countries to establish a geographical context, a conveyor belt for procedures and processes, a funnel if you want to consolidate ideas, a pyramid for a hierarchy.

- **Create connections:** Drawing simple models will help to structure your thoughts in a coherent way and establish connections. On the following pages you will find an overview of models that can be drawn by hand.

- **Familiar but different.** Everyone understands traffic signs – or the play and pause button signs on the remote control. Even better: surprise your audience by turning traditional symbols (e.g. $) or abbreviations (e.g. 't' for time) into pictograms.

- **Sketches are vital.** If you draw while you speak, you direct attention away from yourself and onto your subject. You are no longer standing in front of a jury, you are speaking with the jury about a separate issue.

- **Wrong but strong.** If you draw a crooked line, don't go back and correct it, because the line of your argument will then be interrupted. The same applies if your circles come out looking like eggs. These are abstract illustrations, not works of art.

- **Play Pictionary.** Practice makes perfect.

MODEL LESSON

HOW TO DRAW SCHEMATICALLY

1. **Triangle**
   How or why are A, B and C
   connected?

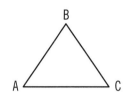

2. **Pie chart**
   How much A and B make C?

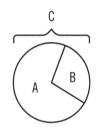

3. **Circle diagram**
   A is followed by B is followed
   by C, and then it starts again
   with A.

4. **Cause-and-effect chain**
   C results from B and B from A.

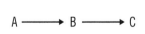

5. **Flowchart or family tree**
   Flowchart: If A, then B or C.
   Family tree: B results from A,
   and C results from A

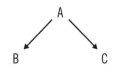

6. Mind map
A makes me think of B and C.
B makes me think of B1, B2, B3.

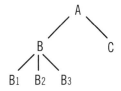

7. Concentric circles
A is part of B is part of C

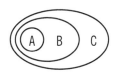

8. Venn diagram
Similarities of A and B, B and C,
C and A, and A, B and C.

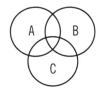

9. Force-field analysis
A contradicts B. C agrees with B.

10. Line chart
The horizontal axis indicates
time (t), the vertical axis Value A.
B and C show progressions (bell
curve, exponential curve, hockey
stick, etc.)

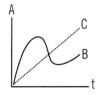

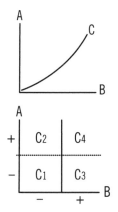

11. Two-dimensional axis model
   (Cartesian coordinates)
   The A and the B axis are different parameters. The curve C shows a possible relationship between the two. Alternative: 4-field matrix. Positions are shown instead of curves.

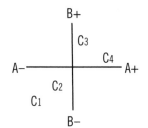

12. Pol model
   The ends of the parameters are opposites: black–white or left–right. Different positions can be shown.

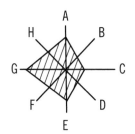

13. Radar chart or Spider
   Shows several parameters which, combined, form a distinctive shape. Good for comparisons.

14. Table

For lists and combinations of
A, B, C and D.

	A	B
C	AC	BC
D	AD	BD

15. Funnel

A and B and C make ...?

16. Bridge

How do we get from A to C if
B is an obstacle?

17. Pyramid

Who tells C what his task is?
Or: How does A legitimise his
position?

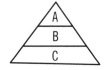

18. Tree

B and C grow out of A.

MY MODELS

BIBLIOGRAPHY

Argyris, Chris; Schön, Donald: *Organizational Learning*. Prentice Hall, 1978

Becker, Udo: *The Continuum Encyclopedia of Symbols*. Continuum, 2000

Bourdieu, Pierre: *Distinction: A Social Critique of the Judgement of Taste*, Harvard University Press, 1984 (Bourdieu model)

Csíkszentmihályi, Mihály: *Creativity: Flow and the Psychology of Discovery and Invention*. Harper Perennial, 1996 (Flow model)

Dijksterhuis, A.; van Olden, Z.: 'On the Benefits of Thinking Unconsciously: Unconscious Thought Can Increase Post-choice Satisfaction', in *Journal of Experimental Social Psychology*, 2006 (Theory of unconscious thinking model)

Douglas, K.; Jones, D.: 'Top 10 Ways to Make Better Decisions', in *New Scientist*, 2 May 2007 (Buyer's decision model)

Drucker, Peter F.: *Managing Oneself*. Harvard Business Press, 2008 (Feedback analysis model)

Elbæk, Uffe: *Kaospilot A-Z*. KaosCommunication, 2003 (Uffe Elbæk model)

Gladwell, Malcolm: *The Tipping Point*. Black Day Books, 2002 (The chasm)

Hersey, P.; Blanchard, K.; Johnson, D.: *Management of Organizational Behavior: Leading Human Resources*. Pearson Education, 2008

Iyengar, S.; Lepper, M.: 'When Choice is Demotivating: Can One Desire Too Much of a Good Thing?', in *Journal of Personality and*

Social Psychology, Vol. 79, 2000 (Jam paradox)

Koch, Richard: *The 80/20 Principle: The Secret of Achieving More with Less.* Doubleday Business, 1997

Kreiner, Kristian; Christensen, Søren: *Projektledelse i løst koblede systemer.* Jurist- og Økonomiforbundets Forlag, 2002 (Consequences model)

Mérö, László: *Moral Calculations: Game Theory, Logic and Human Frailty.* Springer-Verlag New York, 1998 (Prisoner's dilemma)

Mankiw, N. Gregory: *Macroeconomics.* Worth Publishers, 1997

Moeller; Toke; Nissén, Monica: www.interchange.dk (Thinking outside the box)

Morris, Errol: *The Unknown Known*, 2013 (Rumsfeld)

Reason, James: 'Human error: models and management', *British Medical Journal*, 18 March 2000, 320: 768–70 (Swiss cheese)

Schwartz, B.: *The Paradox of Choice: Why More is Less.* Harper Perennial, 2005 (Expectations model)

Stroebe, Wolfgang; Hewstone, Miles; and Stephenson, Geoffrey M.: *Introduction to Social Psychology: A European Perspective.* Blackwell, 1996

Sull, Donald; Eisenhardt, Kathleen: *Simple Rules: How to Thrive in a Complex World.* John Murray, 2015 (Stop Rule; Yes/No Rule)

Taleb, Nassim Nicholas: *The Black Swan: The Impact of the Highly Improbable.* Random House, 2007

Tavris, Carol; Aronson, Elliot: *Mistakes Were Made (But Not by Me).* Harcourt, 2007 (Cognitive dissonance)

Whitmore, John: *Coaching for Performance*, 4th revised edition. Nicholas Brealey Publishing, 2009 (Whitmore model)

https://appreciativeinquiry.case.edu (AI)

http://fiddlerontheproject.wdfiles.com/local--files/start/the balancingact.pdf (Project management triangle)

www.12manage.com/methods_bcgmatrix.html (BCG xox)

www.belbin.com (Role-playing model)

www.grove.com (Drexler/Sibbet)

www.politicalcompass.org (Political compass)

www.sinus-sociovision.de (Sinus Milieu)

www.ted.com/talks/ruth_chang_how_to_make_hard_ choices (Hard choice model)

www.zwicky-stiftung.ch (Morphological box)

THANKS

The writing of this book would not have been possible without the generous help of the following people and institutions:

Pat Ammon, Multiple Global Design (for the Morphological box); Chris Anderson, *Wired* (for the Long tail model); Andrew Anthony (for the assessment of the team model); Andreas 'Becks' Dietrich (for intelligent sparring); Uffe Elbæk (for his ability to draw anything, as well as for the Uffe Elbæk model); Matt Fischer, Apple Music Store (for inspiration); Karin Frick, GDI (for a glimpse into the future); Dag Grœdal, Nordea (for helpful suggestions); Peter Haag (because he believed [in] us); Cédric Hiltbrand (for his corrections); the Kaospilot University (for the best education imaginable); Marc Kaufmann (for positive disrespectfulness); Benno Maggi (for the Gap-in-the-market and Swiss cheese models, as well as for continuous feedback); Christian Nill (for feedback); Courtney Page-Ferell, Play (for the advice 'Don't take yourself too seriously'); Sven Opitz, University of Basel (for Double-loop learning); Louisa Dunnigan and Paul Forty, Profile Books (for great editing and making all of this possible), Jenny Piening (for careful and smart translation), Sara Schindler and Laura Clemens (for editing and proofreading); Pierre-André Schmid, University of Bern (for his ongoing interest and the many books); Ute Tellmann, University of Basel (for criticism of the models); and Daniel Weber, *NZZ Folio* (for helpful advice).

FINAL NOTE

This book is constantly being changed. If you come across mistakes, if you know of other, better models, if you have suggestions of how a model can be further developed, or if you simply want to make a comment, please write to us. You can find our contact details at:

www.rtmk.ch

If you want to know what kind of decision-making type you are, do our little online test:

www.decisiontest.com

THE AUTHORS

Mikael Krogerus is Finnish. He was born in Stockholm and completed his studies in 2003 at the Kaospilot School in Denmark. He went on to work for the youth TV show Chat the Planet in New York, and from 2005 was an editor at *NZZ Folio*, the magazine of the *Neue Zürcher Zeitung*. Since 2015 he has been an editor at *Das Magazin*.

Roman Tschäppeler is Swiss and was born in Bern. He completed his studies at the Kaospilot School in Denmark in 2003 and did a Master's at the Zürcher Hochschule der Künste. He produces films, cultural projects, campaigns and more in his atelier 'guzo': www.guzo.ch.

Philip Earnhart is a freelance art director, artist and designer. In 1989 he completed his studies at the Art Institute of Seattle. He went on to work for design studios and advertising agencies in the USA and Europe. Today he runs his own studio: earnhart.www.earnhart.com.

Jenny Piening is a freelance translator, editor and writer based in Berlin.

This new and revised edition first published in
Great Britain in 2017 by
PROFILE BOOKS LTD
3 Holford Yard
Bevin Way
London WC1X 9HD
www.profilebooks.com

First published in Switzerland by
Kein & Aber AG Zurich

Copyright © 2017 Kein & Aber AG Zurich – Berlin

3 5 7 9 10 8 6 4 2

Printed and bound by
Printed and bound in Italy by L.E.G.O. S.p.A.

A CIP catalogue record for this book is available from the
British Library.

ISBN 978 1 78125 954 2
eISBN 978 1 78283 405 2

**HOW TO IMPROVE
MYSELF**

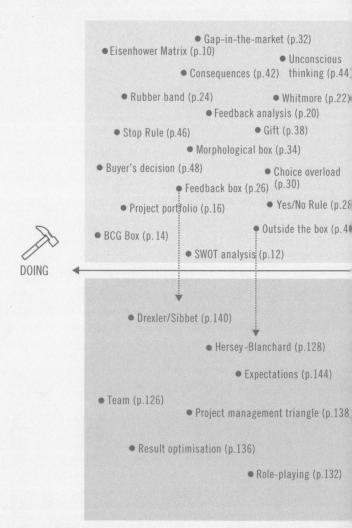

● Gap-in-the-market (p.32)

● Eisenhower Matrix (p.10)

● Unconscious

● Consequences (p.42)   thinking (p.44)

● Rubber band (p.24)   ● Whitmore (p.22)

● Feedback analysis (p.20)

● Stop Rule (p.46)   ● Gift (p.38)

● Morphological box (p.34)

● Buyer's decision (p.48)   ● Choice overload

● Feedback box (p.26)   (p.30)

● Project portfolio (p.16)   ● Yes/No Rule (p.28)

● BCG Box (p. 14)   ● Outside the box (p.40)

● SWOT analysis (p.12)

DOING

● Drexler/Sibbet (p.140)

● Hersey-Blanchard (p.128)

● Expectations (p.144)

● Team (p.126)

● Project management triangle (p.138)

● Result optimisation (p.136)

● Role-playing (p.132)

**HOW TO IMPROVE
OTHERS**